insight text guide

Robert Beardwood & Marlene Drysdale

Stolen

Jane Harrison

First published in 2001, reprinted in 2003, 2004, 2006, 2009, 2015, 2016, 2018, 2020, 2021, 2022, 2024.

Insight Publications Pty Ltd
3/350 Charman Road
Cheltenham VIC 3192
Australia
Tel: +61 3 8571 4950
Email: books@insightpublications.com.au

www.insightpublications.com.au

National Library of Australia Cataloguing-in-Publication entry:
Beardwood, Robert
Insight text guide: Stolen
ISBN 9781875882748
For secondary school age.
Harrison, Jane—Criticism and interpretation.
Harrison, Jane—Stolen.
813.54

Other ISBNs:
9781922525086 (digital)

Cover design: The Modern Art Production Group

Printed by Markono Print Media Pte Ltd

contents

THE CHARACTERS

The characters in this play are five children, all of whom have been placed in the Cranby Children's Home.

Jimmy

Changes from a lively, happy child to a silent, angry, hostile man. Told that his mother is dead but continues to search for her. Abused by the white people he visits as a child. His mother dies before he has a chance to meet her. Hangs himself in a prison cell.

Ruby

Taken from her family at a very early age. Longs for her mother and a loving family. Sexually abused by the white couple she visits as a child. Goes mad and in the end cannot communicate with the family she has yearned for when they make contact with her.

Sandy

Comes into the children's home at an older age. Strongly influenced by his mother and sustained by his memories of her. 'Always on the run.' Moves regularly to avoid the Welfare. Storyteller of the group – keeps the tradition alive for himself and the other children.

Shirley

Strong, comforting presence in the children's home. Her daughter, **Kate**, and son, **Lionel**, are taken from her. Never stops searching for her family. Later finds Kate and re-establishes a relationship with her. Loves being a mother and grandmother.

Anne

Adopted by a well-off white couple and given material comforts. Not close to her white parents. Is shocked when she finds out she is Aboriginal. Torn between both her families, confused about her identity and where she belongs.

OVERVIEW

Introduction

Jane Harrison's play *Stolen* highlights the traumatic experiences of Indigenous Australian children who were removed from their families – children who have come to be known collectively as the Stolen Generations.

Stolen was first staged in a joint production by the Ilbijerri Aboriginal and Torres Strait Islander Theatre Cooperative and Melbourne's Playbox Theatre in March 1997. Since then, *Stolen* has received widespread critical and popular acclaim, both within Australia and internationally.

The issue of the Stolen Generations (initially Generation, singular) is one of the most confronting, and for a long time suppressed, issues in Australia's history. Indigenous children were forcibly removed from their families and communities from the first days of the European occupation of Australia. Almost all Aboriginal families were affected across one or more generations by the removal of children between 1910 and 1970.

When the Human Rights and Equal Opportunity Commission (HREOC) held a national inquiry into the matter in 1995 and 1996, and published their report, *Bringing Them Home*, the destructive effects of the policies of assimilation and segregation were exposed to all.

Stolen's five children have been placed in the Cranby Children's Home. Two of them, Ruby and Jimmy, suffer so deeply that one descends into madness and the other hangs himself in a prison cell. Another child, Anne, is adopted, but for a number of years she has no knowledge or memory of her Aboriginal family. Shirley and Sandy maintain their Aboriginal identities and hope to return to their families. Shirley plays a major role as the mother figure, helping the children to remain strong.

The children are desperate for outside contact, but Ruby and Jimmy return from visits to white families abused, confused and ashamed. Starved of affection, longing for their families, the children are deeply emotionally scarred.

Stolen challenges the stereotypical attitude that the removal of Indigenous children from their families was in the children's best interests. Even today, many of these children still do not know where they come from or which family they belong to. But they understand where they have been and the suffering it caused them. *Stolen* has taken the plight of these children to the world.

An interview with Jane Harrison

Indigenous writer Jane Harrison is a descendant of the Muruwari people of New South Wales. She lives in country Victoria and works on a voluntary basis with Aboriginal youth, developing street drama at Rumbulara Aboriginal Cooperative in Shepparton.

Marlene Drysdale interviewed Jane Harrison for Insight Publications in 2001.

Marlene Drysdale: *I would like you to tell me something about the characters: what is your perception about the characters, firstly Jimmy?*

Jane Harrison: I will just give you an overall idea of the brief that was given to me by Ilbijerri [Aboriginal and Torres Strait Island Theatre Co-operative] because the work was commissioned. They wanted it to be a play that wasn't just one person's story; it showed a range of issues and a range of stories. We came up with the idea of the five different characters and I suppose each of them had a different experience in life, all having had the experience of being taken from their families but the end result of their life varied.

So, Jimmy I saw as being the cheeky kid – pinched the apples because he was hungry. He had a reason for doing it; he wasn't just a bad kid but always positive, the one who was always waiting for someone to come and rescue him. He had a lot of hope, a shining, bright, happy kid who gradually, through life experiences, had that kind of bashed out of him really.

I see him as the kid who first got in trouble as a young boy, maybe for pinching the apples, then the police get involved and then eventually he is the one who ends up incarcerated and continually told in the children's home that his mother doesn't want him, that she's dead, and the light goes out of his life and he ends up just without hope, I suppose. Although, he's still got that kernel of longing to believe. All the time he was told that his mother had died, that part inside him was hoping that she was still alive until, unfortunately, when he is told that his mother is alive and is looking for him. In a short space of time she dies, before they get a chance to meet.

Although that seems almost melodramatic, I found so often in researching the stories that that happened, because it is a fact of life that Indigenous people don't have the life expectancy of non-Indigenous people. So many people had that experience of being reunited taken away from them, so it was a last blow.

M: *The Stolen Generations certainly highlighted a lot of that. Let's talk about Ruby.*

J: Ruby I saw as a child who was taken away at a very early age, as a baby, so she didn't have any mothering experience at all. So she had to kind of imagine that. The play wasn't meant to be set in any particular era but I saw Ruby as being very much a victim of those policies where they took kids away and put them in the missions or the children's home. There they trained them up to be domestics and that was the only expectation that that era of children knew. Then as young thirteen-year-olds they went into the white home, did the domestic work and were probably abused by the family that they were with; that is her story. Again one of a spiral downwards, a spiral into mental illness. When her family finally do locate her, there's really not much left of poor Ruby.

M: *What about Shirley?*

J: Shirley I see as the strong kind, maternal, the earth mother who, even though she was taken away as a child – and I wanted to show the generational thing that children who were taken away often had their children in turn taken away – so even though she had that experience, I think she's got a strength to her, the one who never gives up hope, never stops looking for her children. She can't go back to her mother, that experience is not available to her, but she can keep looking for her children and keep the hope alive. She looks to the future of her grandchildren, so she is a very strong, earthy woman.

M: *She comes across fairly much like that in the play too. Then there was Sandy.*

J: Sandy – I suppose I saw him coming into the children's home at an older age, so he still has a bit of his culture. He's the one who tells a story, he knows a few of the words; he keeps that alive for the other children by telling them the stories and some of the words. He's someone who has had the experience of having been moved on a lot in his life, from an early age trying to keep away from the welfare, and stuff like that. His whole 'arc' as a character is that, finally at the end he wants to go home, back to his place. So he's got a strong connection to the land, I think.

M: *The spirituality is still there. The last character is Anne.*

J: Anne is the one who most resembles me, in a way. Anne is the person who's brought up in a white family, who doesn't even know she's Indigenous – and I think that's what probably happened to a lot of us who have a fairer complexion. Anne discovers that she's got an Aboriginal mother and kind of has to really juggle with that, with what it means to her – her identity – how she feels about the family who adopted her and all those issues about going back and being confused and confronted with a whole lot of people. She doesn't even know which one of them is her mother – that kind of thing, really having to juggle with who she is. At the end of the play she's not really resolved about who she is, but she's had a more positive experience, tied up in neat little bows, [than] any of the characters really.

M: *There was a lot of dislocation in each character's life and I think that's part of that broken jigsaw that we seem to have. When you started to write the play, what was the inspiration to do it?*

J: Well, I didn't come up with the inspiration, actually, Ilbijerri did, so [they] had the idea to work on that theme – at that stage we called it 'The Lost Children' – and they commissioned me to do it. I was someone who had always been aware of my Aboriginal heritage but really didn't know (and that is why I say Anne is a close character to myself) where I fitted in. This was a fantastic opportunity for me to find out what it meant to be Indigenous and make those connections that I'm still trying to make and find out where I belong, because I have this really strong longing to belong in that community. I responded to the ad that Ilbijerri placed and was fortunate enough to get the job of writing. I didn't know it would take six years.

There have been a lot of tears shed along the way but it's been a fantastic experience. They very clearly had the idea for a play about this issue; it was meant to be purely for an Indigenous audience. It was an opportunity to have Indigenous people write, research, act, direct; and it was meant to be presented to the Indigenous community. It was just a lot further along the track when Playbox Theatre Centre heard about it and took it on board and it was right for it to reach a wider audience without (I hope) losing the Koorie audience because they are still the most important for us.

M: *Absolutely. Were you surprised at how successful it has been?*

J: Absolutely blown over really! Because, I suppose, it did take so long, and there were a lot of hiccups along the way, hiccups with funding and workshops – and Ilbijerri were in the position where they had no full-time staff, no artistic director, part-time admin people. People were doing their full-time job and then rolling up for committee meetings and so it was difficult to maintain the energy and keep those submissions going in and write the stuff that funding bodies wanted to hear. So it really did take a long time. I remember them saying to me, 'Oh next year we'll do it, we'll get the funding for it next year'. So it was like, 'Oh yeah'.

I suppose if I'd known it was going to have this much impact I might have put more energy into it, but I might have been scared off completely from doing it. It was a very daunting project. I felt a huge burden of responsibility to the people I was representing. It was very important for all of us that the community would feel it was their play, and the best praise the play's had, people will come up to me and say, 'You got that right, that's my story, I can identify with a bit of it'.

M: *Having seen the play myself, it was, from my perspective (being part of the audience) and being part of the community, an extremely powerful thing. It had an impact on you in the theatre itself, but it had an ongoing impact for weeks. You were still thinking about things that had happened and sounds that were there and various characters and the imagery that was there that you were focused on. But it was like there was a second play in the back of your head that was there ... one instance that I didn't recognise at first was the bed, when Jimmy was lying on the bed, how it represented the bars in the prison and it took me a while to think about what the doll represented with Ruby. So it was all those things; it wasn't a play that you saw and went away from.*

J: I hope not, a lot of the credit for that should be given to Wesley [Wesley Enoch, Director] and the cast coming up with those visual images and those powerful things. For me personally, I find the most powerful part in the play is when the actors tell their story at the end, and that's something that Wesley and the crew and the cast came up with. I joke that the play is almost like a prelude to that part because that, to me, is when it really hits the audience. This isn't something that happened in the past, happened a long time ago, this is now and the effects of it are now.

BACKGROUND & CONTEXT

Stolen: a performance history

The Ilbijerri Aboriginal and Torres Strait Islander Theatre Cooperative commissioned Jane Harrison to write a play about the Stolen Generations in 1992. *Stolen*'s first season was a joint production in Melbourne by Ilbijerri and the Playbox Theatre in March 1997, and another joint production ran as part of the 1998 Melbourne Festival, gaining widespread acclaim.

The return season ran for five weeks in 1999 and also toured regional Victoria. In 2000 the Ilbijerri-Playbox production of *Stolen* was staged in Adelaide, Sydney and Tasmania. Throughout these performances, director Wesley Enoch found the audiences' responses to be emotionally intense:

> It is hard having to live through these stories night after night, to see Aboriginal people, and also white people, sitting in the audience absolutely in tears.[1]

Stolen travelled to London as part of the *HeadsUp: Australian Arts 100* festival in July 2001. Its success at this time led to a return season in London, and five other regional areas in England, in 2001. *Stolen* has played a significant role in making the experiences of the Stolen Generations more widely known in Australia, and also overseas.

The Stolen Generations: a brief history

The removal of Aboriginal children from their families began in the 1800s, and was carried out most systematically between 1910 and 1970. It occurred in tandem with the assimilation policy, officially adopted from 1937, and it often combined the resources and ideologies of governments and churches. The intention was for Aboriginal culture and identity to

---

1 Cited by Penelope Debelle, 'Denial fails to steal play's message', *The Age*, 4 April 2000, p.7.

disappear. Thus Aboriginal children, especially children of mixed-race parentage, were brought up as white members of society and denied contact with their Aboriginal culture and families.

Why the Stolen Generations?

The term 'Stolen Generations' came into widespread use in the early 1980s. In 1981 the non-Aboriginal historian Peter Read was asked to write a pamphlet about the history of separation for the Family and Children's Service Agency in Sydney. This NSW government agency aimed to reduce the instances of separation of Aboriginal children from their families. When Read realised the extent of the policies and practices of separation, he at first thought of the affected children as the 'lost generations'; but his partner suggested to him that those generations were not so much lost as stolen. Read's pamphlet, published by the NSW government in 1981, was therefore titled 'The Stolen Generations'.

The problems faced by the Stolen Generations have proved to be profound, widespread and long lasting. Children placed in institutions were deprived of a supportive, nurturing home environment. Many of them experienced forms of physical, sexual and emotional abuse, both within institutions and within the homes of white families they visited or in their adoptive homes. Although they received some form of Western education, Aboriginal children raised in institutions were expected to take up positions as domestic servants and cleaners, or in other traditionally working-class occupations.

Life in an institution

Aboriginal children were taken from their parents and placed in institutions with little or no contact with their families. The institutions' role was to ensure the children were 'saved' from their 'heathen' ways and turned into good Christians and 'useful' citizens – which in fact meant they were trained as a cheap source of labour for the homes and properties of white people.

In their book *The Lost Children*, Coral Edwards and Peter Read describe a typical daily schedule for children in an institution:

1 The children to be up and dressed by 6 and set to work.
2 To wash themselves by ½ past 7, go to Prayers and breakfast at 8.
3 To work to 10 o'clock.
4 To wash and go to school from 10 till 12, write one copy, read half an hour, cypher [arithmetic/maths] 1 hour.
5 To dine at ¼ after 12 and play till 1.
6 To school at 1, read and cypher till 2.
7 Work from 2 till 6, the boys carpentering and the girls sewing and knitting.
8 To play and wash and be ready for supper at 7.
9 To Prayers at ½ past 7 and be in bed at 8.[2]

This lifestyle was harsh and cold; many children did not know where they were from or what the future held for them. In the words of Margaret Tucker: 'our hearts were absolutely broken'.[3] Another testimonial recalls the living conditions in this way:

> There was no food, nothing. We were all huddled up in a room like a little puppy dog on the floor. Sometimes at night we'd cry with hunger. We had to scrounge in the town dump, eating old bread, smashing tomato sauce bottles, licking them. Half of the time the food we got was from the rubbish dump.[4]

The children, and the families from which they were taken, experienced trauma, loss and dislocation. This has resulted in ongoing problems for Aboriginal people.

In the last twenty or so years, many Aboriginal people have attempted to locate family members with whom they lost contact in childhood due to the policies of separation and assimilation. Some have tried to contact

---

2 Coral Edwards and Peter Read, *The Lost Children*, Doubleday, Moorebank, 1989, p.x.

3 See the video *Lousy Little Sixpence*, dir. Alec Morgan, Ronin Films, 1985.

4 Human Rights and Equal Opportunity Commission (HREOC), *Bringing Them Home*, Stirling Press, Sydney, 1997, p.15.

their own removed children. Sometimes, re-establishing contact with families has been concurrent with identifying as an Aboriginal person for the first time.

Contemporary issues and politics

In 1995 and 1996, the Human Rights and Equal Opportunities Commission conducted a national inquiry into the removal of Aboriginal children from their families. The inquiry was led by Ronald Wilson and Mick Dodson, and the report *Bringing Them Home: the report of the national inquiry into the separation of Aboriginal and Torres Strait Islander children from their families* was tabled in Federal Parliament in 1997. Since then, *Bringing Them Home* and the issue of the Stolen Generations have been keenly analysed and debated in the media, by politicians, and in Australian society generally.

Some of the debate has focused on the appropriateness of the term 'Stolen Generations'. Sometimes the singular form 'generation' has been used, although this implies that only one generation of Aboriginal people was affected or separated, which is incorrect. An objection from members of the conservative Howard government (1996–2007) and some sections of the mass media was that the term 'stolen' was inappropriate, insofar as it (allegedly) exaggerated the actual historical events and circumstances.

In April 2000, former Aboriginal Affairs minister John Herron wrote a submission to the senate 'inquiry into the Stolen Generation', in which he claimed that 'there was never a generation of stolen children' because not *all* children from a given generation were removed.[5] Herron's claim was strongly criticised by Aboriginal leaders, the Australian Labor Party, the Australian Democrats, and some members of the Liberal Party. However, former Prime Minister John Howard supported Herron's statement.

The debate flared up again in February 2001, when the former head of ATSIC (the Aboriginal and Torres Strait Islander Commission), Lowitja O'Donoghue, was reported in the *Herald Sun* newspaper as saying that

5 See *The Age*, 4 April 2000 for a number of articles on this.

the word 'removed' rather than stolen was more appropriate to her own childhood experience of being placed in an institution. The journalist concerned, Andrew Bolt, had for several years been referring to the set of issues and events relating to the Stolen Generations as the 'Stolen Generations myth'. His article was not only strongly biased against O'Donoghue, misrepresenting what she had actually said to him in an interview, but enabled members of the former coalition government, particularly former Prime Minister Howard, to reaffirm their opposition to the use of the term 'stolen'.

The issue of an apology

Australia's former Prime Minister, John Howard, was criticised by many Indigenous leaders and community leaders during his term of office for refusing to comply with one of the chief recommendations of the *Bringing Them Home* report, that the Australian government apologise to Aboriginal people for the removal of children from families and communities. It seems that the issue of compensation to Aboriginal people lay behind this refusal to apologise, although this has been obscured by other aspects of the debate such as the question of the appropriateness of the word 'stolen' and the question of whether current generations of Australians or a current Australian government is responsible for the actions of former leaders and citizens. Interestingly, Howard's refusal has been an element of a more popular pro-reconciliation movement, which includes recognition of and participation in the National Sorry Day (26 May, since 1998).

On 13 February 2008, John Howard's successor, Kevin Rudd, said 'sorry' to the Aboriginal people of Australia in a groundbreaking speech to the Australian Parliament. Speaking of 'removing a stain from the soul of Australia', he apologised 'For the pain, suffering and hurt of these Stolen Generations, their descendants and for their families left behind'.[6]

---

6 See www.aph.gov.au/hansard/reps/dailys/dr130208.pdf for a transcript of the Apology.

The case for compensation

In August 2000, the Federal Court tried and rejected a case brought against the Commonwealth Government by two Northern Territory members of the Stolen Generations, Peter Gunner and Lorna Cubillo. Justice O'Loughlin found insufficient evidence that 'a general removal policy had ever existed'.[7] However, academic Robert Manne's assessment of the evidence considered by Justice O'Loughlin arrives, persuasively, at the opposite conclusion. In 2001 there were more than 2100 compensation claims pending in the courts.[8] Despite his apology of 2008, Kevin Rudd asserted that, 'We will not, under any circumstances, be establishing any compensation arrangements or any compensation fund.'[9]

Aboriginal theatre: a political tradition

Stolen makes the connections between its *fictitious* representations of Aboriginal people and the social and political *realities* of their lives much more obvious and significant than connections between fiction and reality in mainstream theatre usually are. This is consistent with political nature of Aboriginal theatre.

Aboriginal theatre did not emerge until the late 1960s. The first Aboriginal writer for the stage was Kevin Gilbert, whose play *The Cherrypickers* was written in 1968 and then workshopped at Sydney's Mews Theatre in 1971. Robert Merritt followed with *The Cakeman*, which in 1978 became the first play by an Aboriginal playwright to be published. In 1982, two of Jack Davis' plays were performed for the first time: *Kullark* and *The Dreamers*. They were followed in 1984 by *No Sugar*, and in 1988 by *Barungin (Smell the Wind)*.

The Eora Centre for the Performing Arts was established in Sydney in 1984. In 1987, the first National Black Playwright's Conference was held

7 Robert Manne, *The Age*, 2 September 2000, Extra pp.1–2.

8 *The Weekend Australian*, 26–27 May 2001, p.4.

9 www.abc.net.au/am/content/2008/s2152790.htm

in Canberra, demonstrating that Aboriginal theatre was more than just a token gesture. The influential academic and critic of Aboriginal literature, Adam Shoemaker, suggests that

> the distinctiveness of black Australian plays is thrown into clear relief when it is contrasted with largely unsuccessful efforts of other playwrights ... who fail to penetrate the Aboriginal worldview.[10]

An 'Aboriginal worldview' is represented and evoked in Aboriginal theatre through a number of technical features, which we will now consider in relation to *Stolen*.

---

10 Adam Shoemaker, *Black Words White Page: Aboriginal Literature 1929–1988*, University of Queensland Press, St Lucia, 1992, p.249.

GENRE, STRUCTURE & LANGUAGE

The genre of Aboriginal theatre: some characteristics

One characteristic of Aboriginal theatre is its use of traditional Aboriginal culture. In particular, the Dreamtime myths provide a rich source of story and drama. In *Stolen* the use of myth can be seen through the character of Sandy, who tells the story of the Mungee and the story of the creation of the desert sands.

The children do not form a passive audience for Sandy's stories, but actively take part. The Aboriginal approach towards storytelling and 'theatre' is one of a shared, community experience, rather than one that rigidly separates performers and audience.

Language and silence

Another feature of Aboriginal theatre is the use of Aboriginal language or speech idioms. For instance, Jack Davis' *Barungin* includes a glossary of Aboriginal terms, and the reader's attention is drawn to these words in the published text by their being italicised.[11]

An interesting stylistic feature of *Stolen* is its economical use of language, and its emphasis on gesture and facial expression. Silence is often as important as speech in communicating meaning or the experience of extremely intense emotions. A good example of this is Shirley's scene 'It rained the day', in which the stage direction indicates: *'her grief cannot be expressed in words'* (p.9). Instead, her feelings are communicated through her body language and her action of clinging on to her baby's tiny jumper.

The use of Aboriginal language is less a feature of *Stolen* than in other Aboriginal theatre. This reflects the fact that, in the Cranby Children's Home, the children are forbidden to use Aboriginal words. The removal

---

11 Jack Davis, *Barungin: Smell the Wind*, Currency, Sydney, 1989.

of Aboriginal children from their families is thus placed in the context not of the government's concern for their material wellbeing, but of a larger, racist government project that attempted to silence and then eventually destroy Aboriginal culture.

Humour

In his comprehensive critical study of Aboriginal literature, Mudrooroo notes that a 'self-deprecating humour permeates the dialogue of just about all the Indigenous plays I have seen or read'.[12] The role of humour in *Stolen* is very important, since the play represents so many distressing events and has, overall, a serious tone and message. In fact, the play's message is more effectively communicated *because* the theatrical experience is not all on the same emotional level.

The characters' ability to laugh at their own predicaments is a feature of their resilience, of their collective capacity to survive oppressive governmental and bureaucratic regimes. The children's use of white speech patterns often turns into mimicry and parody, as in their chants and games – patty cake, for instance, or the tune 'We're Happy Little Vegemites'. These occasions partly alleviate the children's sufferings as a result of abuse, or when they realise that their work prospects are little better than slave labour.

Shirley 'laughs bitterly' at being put on hold on the phone, realising it is an apt metaphor for how bureaucratic systems have been treating her 'for twenty-seven years' (p.22). Later, Sandy laughs at the thought of buying a luxury apartment in the refurbished children's home (p.32). Sandy's laughter provides an important moment of relief, amidst the trauma and loss represented in the scenes immediately before and after. The moment of humour, though, still allows an important point to be made – that places can be remade in such a way as to erase the signs of their previous use, and to hide truths that those in positions of power may want to prevent from coming to light.

---

12 Mudrooroo, 'Our World a Stage', in *Milli Milli Wangka: the Indigenous Literature of Australia*, Hyland House, Melbourne, 1997, p.160.

Stolen's frequent touches of humour and irony also suggest a possible mode of Aboriginal resistance to white culture. In this form of cultural resistance, the meaning of ordinary language is transformed, and words that in certain contexts seem innocent are invested with more sinister overtones.

For instance, the song 'We're Happy Little Vegemites' is performed by the children in the scene 'Cleaning routine 2' (pp.17–19), and the irony of its concluding line – 'It puts a rose in every cheek' – turns the light-hearted routine into a critique of white authority. The 'rose in every cheek' is not due to the children's genuine happiness in performing their tasks, but due to their strenuous physical exertions for the benefit of their white 'employers'. The use of irony enables the severely restricted opportunities available to the children to be dealt with in a comic mode, mocking any suggestion that these opportunities will somehow turn the children into happy and productive members of society.

Non-chronological structure

The structure of *Stolen* is relatively loose, dispensing with the conventional theatrical divisions of numbered acts and scenes. Such divisions in traditional European theatre serve to order the flow of time and invest the events being dramatised with a sense of coherence and meaning. However, *Stolen* is about events that have traumatic effects, events that cause the characters' lives to *lack* structure and coherence. The play, like the turmoil experienced by the children, is not set in a fixed, historical time but moves in and out of the past and the present.

Key point

Stolen's short scenes and quick transitions between scenes, with few obvious causal links between them, generate a sense of incoherence. This dramatises and communicates Aboriginal experiences of white oppression, and makes the audience – which, in the case of mainstream Australian theatre, is mostly non-Aboriginal – active participants in the experience of dislocation.

The many temporal shifts within the play are consistent with an Aboriginal view of time. The distinction between past and present is fluid rather than absolute, and the past is never entirely left behind, but continues to inform the present.

Settings, staging and lighting

The minimal use of sets and props in *Stolen* highlights some important themes. The walls of the institution are cold and regimented; the starkness of the dormitory reflects the emptiness in the lives of the children. As soon as there is a glimmer of light or hope it is, like a candle, snuffed out: '*lights fade to black*' is a very frequent stage direction throughout the play.

However, at the play's end the stage is much more strongly lit. Shirley's final speech is delivered with her standing '*in a beam of light at the front of the stage*' (p.35). Rather than end the play with the stage lights fading out and the actors leaving at the rear of the stage, *Stolen* requires the actors to address the audience directly and then leave '*by way of the front of the stage*' (p.36), in light rather than darkness. The use of light thus symbolises the persistence of hope for Aboriginal people, despite their far-too-common experiences of dark despair, suffering and loss.

Audience involvement

The audience's senses are directly involved through the playing of music and the use of Phenol (carbolic acid) in the two 'cleaning routines' (pp.3, 17). This pungent smell bridges the gap between actors and audience, lessening the white audience's (potentially comfortable) sense of distance from the events played out on stage. Of course, Aboriginal audiences have been appreciative of *Stolen* too – in some cases, the play's smells, sights and sounds elicit strong, painful memories of very similar experiences in the lives of Aboriginal audience members.

SCENE-BY-SCENE ANALYSIS

Arriving (p.1)

This scene is a prelude or introduction to the play. Its only scripted words are Ruby's 'My mum's coming for me', signalling the transition into 'Adult flashes'. The actors enter into their roles as children in ways that are visible on stage – by improvised gestures and speech. These shifts *into* character are mirrored at the play's end by the actors' shifts *out* of character, reverting to 'themselves'.

These shifts into and out of character roles help to partially break down the 'illusion' of the stage, and to emphasise the relationship between the play's representations and social realities. The audience is made aware that, although the performers are 'acting', the experiences being dramatised are very close to the experiences of many Aboriginal people during the twentieth century.

Adult flashes (pp.1–2)

This scene is a series of statements from the five main characters as adults; they address the audience rather than each other. The statements refer to events that occur much later in the characters' lives than most of the events of *Stolen*. In this way, 'Adult flashes' provides glimpses of *Stolen*'s own ending, though without divulging its most complicated or traumatic details.

The birth of Shirley's granddaughter, and Shirley's obvious excitement, generate a tone of optimism – balancing, to some extent, the signs of anger, despair and loss already evident in this scene. The way in which the bars of Jimmy's bed appear to be the bars of a prison cell is one way in which an ominous tone is produced. Ruby's loss of sanity is evident from the start. *Stolen*'s later incidents focus on moments much earlier in Ruby's life, showing the causes of her madness.

[Cleaning routine 1] (p.3)

Although this scene is not titled in the script, it is later echoed and developed in 'Cleaning routine 2' (pp.17–19). The audience's senses are involved directly through the playing of music and the use of Phenol. This pungent smell bridges the gap between actors and audience, lessening the audience's (comfortable) sense of distance from the events played out on stage and making them participants rather than spectators. The characters' cleaning routine also represents one example of the kind of manual labour that will be their main form of work later in life.

Hiding Sandy (pp.3–4)

Sandy's childhood movements between members of his extended family are sketched in this scene. In the background is 'the Welfare', the force that motivates the family's anxieties about Sandy and drives his frequent relocations. Sandy's repeated 'Always on the run' is like a chant, reinforcing his inability to escape from a life based on evasion and flight. He continually changes his place of residence, but nevertheless his life circumstances keep repeating themselves.

It rained the day (pp.4–5)

The rain prompts Shirley, as a child in the children's home, to recall being driven in a 'big and black' car away from her mother. This adds to the knowledge, provided in 'Adult flashes', that Shirley's own daughter and son, Kate and Lionel, were also stolen.

The second part of this scene also entails a character's 'flashback' to a much earlier time. Jimmy acts out a childhood incident in the chook yard and his mother's voice (offstage) warns him about the Welfare. He shifts, for a moment, into his adult character, before waking as a child. This brief scene juxtaposes Jimmy's adult and child personalities; it blends dream and memory, present and past.

Line-up 1 (pp.5–6)

The children line up so that one of them can be chosen for a weekend visit to a white couple's home. The children appear completely powerless in the process of selection, although they *'sell themselves in their own particular way'* (p.6). The white characters who play such significant roles in the children's lives remain shadowy, and their own personalities or reactions are completely invisible to the children – and to the audience, too. In this scene, whiteness is present only in the form of the white spotlight that picks out Ruby, and it makes her look white too. The significance of skin colour is also evident in the line-up sequence, whereby the stage direction indicates that the line should be made twice, to draw the audience's attention not just to this selection factor, but also to the children's consciousness of it.

The chosen (pp.6–7)

Anne – the one who is 'chosen' – appears to have a very uneasy and distant relationship with her white parents. Although they speak to her, she does not speak to them but addresses the audience directly. She appears very alone and isolated, in comparison with her scenes in the children's home.

The parents are represented by *'shadows falling on to a Venetian blind or a white sheet'* (p.6), and by offstage voices. A white spotlight falls on Anne, while her parents appear dark. Anne has already forgotten the children's home and obediently says her prayers. This scene represents events that occur later in Anne's life than the scenes that follow in the play – another example of Harrison's flexibility with time. Episodes from Anne's life in the children's home are alternated throughout *Stolen* with episodes from her life with her white parents.

Jimmy being naughty (pp.7–8)

Jimmy steals apples from an orchard; the others eat them. A lot of meaning is communicated in the stage direction: '*The others all eat apples as if they've never tasted one before*' (p.7). The implication of this direction is that, for the children, stealing food is largely a matter of obtaining enough to eat; even something as common as an apple is novel and precious to them. The audience must assume that the orchard owner is white. Like most of the other white characters, he is unseen and only heard as a threatening, forbidding voice. Jimmy is the ringleader here, emphasising his spirited personality as a child.

Unspoken abuse 1 (p.8)

The children eagerly greet Ruby on her return. They play the 'patty cake game' and chant a series of questions, a playful way of broaching the question of a secret. This secret takes on a sinister quality when its unspeakable nature becomes evident. The children cease the chant and their clapping when Ruby admits she has 'promised not to tell'. Ruby's silence on this matter seems to have been bought by the 'gift' of a doll.

It rained the day (p.9)

As in the earlier scene, Shirley's memories are triggered by the sound of rain. Here, though, Shirley appears as her adult self. What Shirley experiences as a child she later relives as a mother, equally powerless in the face of the Welfare. This overlapping of childhood and adult experiences is reinforced in *Stolen* by the overlapping of times: Shirley's 'adult' scenes are interspersed with scenes in which the characters are all children in the home together (such as 'Unspoken abuse 1').

Key point

Repetition and entrapment: The repetition of the scene title 'It rained the day', and of key phrases – such as 'that big black car', echoing the earlier 'the car's big and black' (p.4) – reflects how entrapped the lives of Aboriginal people became as a result of the government policies of assimilation, segregation, and the removal of Indigenous children from their families.

Like Ruby's experience of abuse, Shirley's feelings *'cannot be expressed in words'*. Only the barest outline of events is given in Shirley's short speech. The stage directions *'gesturing for her husband'* and *'crumples back down on the bed'* indicate how her deep-seated emotions must be conveyed by the actor's facial gestures and body language. Also, the baby's jumper is significant, since it represents Shirley's desire to hold onto something tangible, something that stands in for her actual family members in their continuing absence.

Ruby comforting her baby (pp.9–10)

Ruby's 'baby' is the doll given to her on a weekend visit. She calls the doll 'Ruby' and speaks to it as a mother, before slipping back into her child identity. This is an early sign of Ruby's instability, and it is clearly related to the lack of a caring, nurturing mother in her life. This and Ruby's inability to recover her mother's presence (or a loving substitute) prompt her despairing cry, recurrent throughout the play: 'Where are you?'. When Ruby throws the doll to the floor, there is a deeper resonance: the doll is as easily discarded as these children have been by white society.

Sandy's story of the Mungee (pp.10–11)

Sandy brings the children together by telling this story. Sandy's links to traditional Aboriginal culture are stronger than those of the other children. This is indicated by his use of an Aboriginal word, 'yurringa'. Shirley protests: 'you're not allowed to say that' (p.10), which explains why Aboriginal words are so rare in the play. However, Sandy persists, and the children are drawn into the story to the extent of acting out roles in it. The story narrates a tribe's encounters with a black creature, the Mungee, which steals and eats children in the night. The tribal elders eventually capture the Mungee by turning it white with 'magic powdered bone' (p.11).

The threat of darkness and invisibility is thus overcome with whiteness, but the irony is that white people have been removing black children from their families in broad daylight. The loaded, racial meanings of 'black' and 'white', and the reversal of the conventional childhood 'fear of the dark', are emphasised once more at the scene's end, as Sandy warns Ruby that 'it's not the dark you need to be afraid of' (p.11).

Your mum's dead (pp.11–13)

Jimmy's humour and rebelliousness are now succeeded by his distress and loneliness. His oppression takes two forms: he is beaten, and communication with his mother, Nancy Wajurri, is obstructed. The Matron tells Jimmy that his mother is dead, but Nancy's onstage presence clearly shows the audience that the Matron is lying, and that Jimmy's intuition is correct. Despite the blocked communication, Jimmy and Nancy never give up hope of re-establishing their relationship.

Nancy's letters help to give *Stolen* a more precise historical frame. They reveal that Jimmy's childhood incarceration in the Cranby Children's Home is during the 1960s. This is just after Sandy leaves it, in 1958 – a date established later, in the scene 'Sandy's life on the road' (p.25). And it is just before Shirley's son is taken from her in 1966 – established in 'Shirley never gives up searching' (p.21). These dates reflect the historical fact that Aboriginal children were removed over several decades, across several generations.

While Nancy reads out the letters, Jimmy's experiences in the children's home are shown in visual form, in silence except for the *'sound of the strap being applied'* (p.12). Note the use of the children's song about 'Worms that squiggle and squirm' (p.12). Ordinarily this song would suggest a sense of childhood play and innocence. However, in this context it generates a note of self-pity and pathos, since the children are as powerless and persecuted as worms tortured by children. Jimmy is no longer mischievous, as in 'It rained the day', but is now wistful and melancholy.

Line-up 2 (p.13)

The repetition of scene titles and incidents continues the theme of entrapment and powerlessness. The children learn from their collective experiences, hence their apprehension about what will happen to them. In contrast to 'Line-up 1' when they all looked '*eager*' (p.6), now it is only Jimmy who '*looks expectant*' (p.13). Despite their increased knowledge about what is in store for them, they lack the capacity to change things. Jimmy's eagerness to please contrasts with his own later experiences and change in attitude towards those in authority.

Anne's told she's Aboriginal (pp.13–14)

For the first and only time, Anne speaks directly to her white parents, in response to their telling her about her Aboriginal mother. However, the conversation only seems to increase the distance between them.

This scene shows how dramatically different the issues are for the parents compared to Anne, and how any meaningful communication between them is prevented by the parents' prejudice and racism. The main concern of the parents appears to be that Anne's mother is Aboriginal; her white mother suggests 'no one need ever know' and then sobs, 'the shame ...' (p.14). Anne does not understand what it is that is shameful, but she is angry and upset that this knowledge – including (and especially) the fact that her birth mother is alive – has been kept from her.

Unspoken abuse 2 (p.15)

This is another repeated scene, including a reprise of the patty-cake game, with the same conclusion. A link between Ruby and Jimmy is established here, when Jimmy – who seems to be the only one not to have understood that Ruby's experiences include some form of abuse – steals her present, a 'pitcha book'.

Your mum's dead (pp.15–16)

This scene is a near repeat of the earlier scene with the same title. On this occasion, the letter's later date – '8 August, 1966' (p.16) – gives a sense of time moving on in the characters' lives; Nancy describes the increasing hardship of the Wajurri family. Her promise to knit socks for Jimmy generates a link between her and Shirley, who also 'knits for her family' (p.19). The two characters are played by the same actor.

Once again, the filing cabinet is slammed shut, a metaphor for the role of bureaucracy in the destruction of Aboriginal families. The workings of bureaucracy are shown to be completely inaccessible to Aboriginal people, so it can control all the communications between family members who are separated by the Welfare. Despite this, Jimmy still believes his mother is alive. This belief sustains him throughout his years of institutionalisation, first in the children's home and later in prison.

To tan or not to tan (p.16)

Anne considers her *'milky-white skin'*. Her speech highlights the tension between, on one hand, the perceived attractiveness of a suntanned white body – the darkness of which is only skin-deep – and on the other hand, Anne's anxieties about identifying as 'black'. She puts off seeing her *'real* mother' because of her exams and the upcoming 'holiday to Surfers'. That is, Anne's lifestyle choices coincide with those of a conventional white teenager at the end of her school years.

A note of humour is present in this scene due to the pun on Hamlet's famous speech, beginning 'To be or not to be, that is the question'.[13] Hamlet's speech is usually interpreted as concerned with the question of suicide – by comparison with which, Anne's question about acquiring a tan seems much more trivial. However, the issue of a more deep-seated identity as it relates to skin colour and race gives the scene a seriousness of its own.

Shirley's memories (p.17)

Once again, Shirley is the central character in a scene in which she has very few words to say: just 'No! No!'. Whereas in 'It rained the day' (p.9) she is an adult, here she is a child, looking at an old photo album. A projector screens images in order for the audience to participate in the viewing. There is no narrative to connect the images, so they remain fragmented, unexplained and unconnected signs of Shirley's past and her family. Thus the audience is simultaneously included in the viewing and excluded from Shirley's private remembrances – which would provide the 'meaning' of the images. The other characters crowd around Shirley and try to take the album from her, but she resists, clinging onto what little she has left of her past.

Line-up age twelve (p.17)

This scene has another line-up from which Ruby is picked. Shirley seems to know much more than the other children, and she answers Sandy's questions about the prospects for whoever is chosen. In this case, instead of adopting one of the children, the white couple is looking to acquire a maid. The chances of receiving payment for this work appear slim; Shirley's 'Ya meant to ...' indicates both the condition of slavery facing these children and also their awareness of its injustice. The bucket and mop that crash into Ruby's arms following her selection simply fall from

---

13 William Shakespeare, *Hamlet*, Act 3 Scene 1.

above, reinforcing the remote, faceless nature of white power over these children. This also provides a neat transition to the following scene.

Cleaning routine 2 (pp.17–19)

The children all perform their cleaning routine (as indicated in the stage directions at the top of p.3), sweeping and scrubbing the floor. They play the children's game 'what are you going to be when you grow up', but the humorous qualities of this scene, which turns into a song-and-dance number, coexist with a much more serious tone. Professions that are well paid and with high social status, such as those of doctor or engineer, or even of teacher or nurse, are simply unavailable: 'No!' declares the 'authority figure' in the game. But the question of becoming a cleaner or a domestic receives a definite 'Yes!'

The song 'We're Happy Little Vegemites' is used but, instead of being invested with its familiar childlike innocence, the song displays the children's full awareness that society regards them as little more than slave labour. Moreover, the words 'we love to work like slaves' (pp.18, 19) indicate that the children realise that they are expected to be grateful for their status as slaves – poorly paid (if at all), uneducated and given physically demanding duties. The scene's use of irony and humour exposes the exploitation of these children and ridicules any notion that the children's home is genuinely concerned about their 'welfare'.

Ruby's words as she mops the floor at the end of the scene, 'Sorry, ma'am' (p.19), are an apology for no apparent reason. This suggests that, in her position as maid, Ruby quickly grows used to being blamed and scolded. This theme is taken up in the later scene, 'Ruby's descent into madness' (pp.24–5).

Shirley knits for her family (p.19)

Shirley never gives up hope, as represented by her continual knitting of clothes as presents for her family, even though she has had no chance to give them. Her hope is finally rewarded at the end of *Stolen*, but in the early scenes the garments Shirley knits are, along with the photo album, the only tangible signs of her family she has to hold on to. Therefore they are also signs of the hope she invests in her family, but they offer no real security or reassurance.

A can of peas (pp.19–20)

Sandy's story makes an ironic comment about the Welfare's efforts to 'assist' Aboriginal families. These efforts are made to appear tokenistic and hypocritical, since they disguise a deeper prejudice and a lack of respect and compassion towards Aboriginal people. The quality of the food provided by the Welfare is poor. Note the repetition of the adjective 'white' in Sandy's list of the food items: 'White flour, white sugar, white bread' (p.19). This cleverly aligns the foods with the government's racist assimilation policies towards Aboriginal people. The can of peas, the Welfare's 'gift', was found at the back of a cupboard, past its use-by date. It thus turns out, ironically, to be the decisive 'weapon' with which the Welfare destroys Sandy's family.

Jimmy's being naughty again (p.20)

This scene is a turning point in the characterisation of Jimmy. Although his age is not specified, he is out of the children's home and now in danger of being in trouble with the police. Unlike the earlier scene in which he is cheerfully stealing apples and sharing them with the other children, in this scene Jimmy is alone and he is seen to be more resentful than previously. His changed attitude is conveyed through gesture – he is *'looking guiltily around all the time'* – and the tone of his laughter, which is now *'more an angry laugh'*.

Line-up 3 (pp.20–1)

In this scene, Jimmy's childhood personality contrasts dramatically with his appearance in the previous scene. Jimmy's innocence and willingness to please – 'I do what I'm told' (p.21) – make him stand out from the other children. Shirley's warnings do not affect him; like the other children, he learns from bitter experience.

Shirley never gives up searching (pp.21–2)

An adult Shirley attempts to discover the whereabouts of her son, Lionel. She phones various offices, and the other characters help her by ringing on her behalf. However, their combined efforts are met with the bureaucracy's combined denials and deferrals. Although this is an important scene showing the characters banding together, their lack of success leaves Shirley isolated and frustrated, picked out on stage by the spotlight. Shirley is put on hold; she realises this is a metaphor for how she has been treated by white bureaucracy and authority for 'twenty-seven years' – and there is no relief from this situation in sight.

Desert sands (pp.22–3)

As in 'Sandy's story of the Mungee', this story from Sandy is prompted by his desire to cheer up Ruby. Once again, the other characters gather around and become actors in the story, though they leave Sandy to finish the story alone. Unlike the others, Sandy has a strong sense of where he has come from, and 'Desert sands' is the story of his origins. It is not, however, about a pure origin that fits romantic stereotypes about Aboriginal nomads at home in the desert. Instead, the 'old days' Sandy refers to are the times when Aboriginal women 'would shove sand inside themselves. Anything to stop the men from raping them' (p.23). This form of defence does not save Sandy's mother, however, which is the real reason he is named 'Sandy'. His name is thus a continual reminder not just of a place in the desert 'where my people come from' but of the violent treatment of Aboriginal women by white men.

Unspoken abuse 3 (p.23)

Jimmy returns from his weekend visit, and his experience of abuse is expressed through his silence throughout the scene. Ruby stays apart from the action, but the other three children play the patty-cake game, asking the questions and making up the answers until they come to the last one, 'What did he do to ya?'. Jimmy's silence marks a dramatic shift from his previous behaviour in the children's home, and leads to his isolation from the others. Jimmy's aloneness is emphasised by Shirley's action '*to put her arm around him*' which is not completed.

Ruby's descent into madness (pp.24–5)

This is the first of several scenes representing important aspects of the characters' lives after they leave the children's home. For Ruby, the patterns of abuse and despair established in the home are self-perpetuating in her later life. The scene begins with Ruby being beaten; then a number of anonymous authority figures issue orders to her. It is clear that, in Ruby's relationships with these figures, she is no more than a slave who will never meet with her masters' approval.

At first, Ruby interjects from time to time, demonstrating a degree of resistance and independence: 'Don't need no family of me own' (p.24), she declares. However, the voices 'crowd in on her' and she is then silent until the end of the scene. Her scream, 'Where are you?' (p.25) recalls her childhood cries for her mother – indicating that nothing has really changed for Ruby. Her sense of alienation has intensified, though, and it now overwhelms her. The arrival of the ambulance signals a new phase in Ruby's lifetime of institutional care.

Sandy's life on the road (pp.25–6)

Sandy talks to a woman while they wait at a bus stop. In this way he sketches an account of around thirteen years of his life since leaving the children's home in 1958. Like Ruby, Sandy has experienced paid work as exploitative, physically demanding and poorly paid. As an Indigenous worker, he has also experienced the racist practice of receiving inferior wages.

The most striking feature of his life, though, is its restlessness, resulting not from any inherent weakness in Sandy, but always from external factors. He leaves a trawling job because his pay, even after eight years, is less than that of his non-Aboriginal coworkers; on another occasion, the local police make him move on. The stereotype of the Aboriginal person as nomad, inherently unreliable and prone to go 'walkabout' at any moment, receives an implicit critique here. Sandy's mobility is virtually forced on him by social and material circumstances; his *own* desire is to 'settle down. Maybe get myself a family ...' (p.26). In contrast to the injustice of his boss on the trawler, and the ruthlessness of the police who 'moved me on' (p.26), Sandy is extremely adaptable, reliable and resourceful.

Jimmy's story (pp.26–8)

This scene raises the real possibility that Jimmy and his mother will be reunited. Jimmy has been in prison but is now out; his mother's letter indicates that she still believes him to be in the children's home or in a foster home – another sign of how effectively the Welfare has prevented communication between mother and son.

Jimmy goes to a bar that is clearly in the area that his family is from, since he is recognised as 'one of Nancy's boys' (p.27). He does not want to admit his own ignorance, and sticks to what he has been told – that his mother is dead – but quickly realises that the man at the bar is telling the truth. Jimmy recalls his childhood and his capture by the Welfare. His mother contributes to the scene through voice-overs, as Jimmy reflects on and makes sense of his history now that his identity, in a sense, is returned to him. He is now in a position to find his mother.

Am I black or white? (pp.28–9)

Anne describes meeting her Aboriginal mother and family. Her confused sense of identity is represented by the many competing voices and attitudes in this scene. Two voices are those of her father and mother; the three black voices are of unidentified members of her Aboriginal family.

Anne makes a short speech at the start of the scene, describing her expectations of how and where her Aboriginal family would be living, and the disappointing reality: 'they were in a Housing Commission flat, all crowded in' (p.28). After this, she says nothing as the other voices, black and white, clamour for her attention. At first, both families claim an exclusive right to Anne, as if she should belong to one family – and, by implication, one race – only. Anne's confusion is represented by her inability to answer, as she runs from one side of the stage to the other. Finally, the voices merge into each other, saying the same thing: 'Who do you think you are?' (p.29). This is precisely the question Anne is least able to answer.

What do you do? (pp.29–30)

Anne's sense of confusion in 'Am I black or white?' flows into 'What do you do?',which returns to Jimmy and Nancy Wajurri's quest to meet again after twenty-six years of separation and pain. Both are coming to terms with the new, strange prospect of seeing each other and the possibility of disappointment. As Jimmy's mother suggests, 'Maybe we'll be like strangers' (p.29).

Running through this scene is the theme of a birthday celebration. For Jimmy, the twenty-six missed Christmases and birthdays represent the impossibility of catching up on so much experience that ought to have been shared. In fact, he does not even know the date of his mother's birthday. For Nancy, the twenty-six presents represent all that she has wanted to give her son, but has been prevented from giving. The box of presents is unpacked and repacked twice, showing that the gifts are perpetually unable to make the final connection between giver and receiver.

Stereotypes of blackness

Jimmy and Nancy are so unknown to each other that they imagine each other in terms of stereotypical notions of what black people are like. Jimmy wonders if his mother will bring 'all the rellies' (p.30) to live with him, invoking the stereotype of overcrowded houses (a stereotype that can, of course, reflect the real living conditions of Aboriginal families). Nancy, in contrast, wonders if Jimmy will be 'one of those flash blacks with a mobile phone' (p.30). The reality, evident from their sharing the stage, side by side, even though they cannot hear each other, is that their anxieties and desires are very similar. For both mother and son, being with each other once again is far more important than anything else.

When Nancy dies, Jimmy remains unknowing. He seems to have recovered something of his childhood self, as he *'stands happily'* (p.30) and looks forward to the reunion – that the audience now knows will never take place. Jimmy's words at the close of the scene, 'I'm finally going to meet my mother', are ironic because of what the audience knows and Jimmy does not. The scene thus ends at the most poignant moment possible.

Ruby's family come to visit (pp.30–1)

While Ruby has been yearning for her absent mother, until this scene there is no indication that she actually has a family. Ruby's mother never appears in *Stolen*, but with the entry of her father, Len, and her sister, Joanie, the possibility is raised, quite suddenly, that Ruby has a home and a family to go to.

In the previous scene, the audience hopes that Jimmy's search for his mother will have a happy outcome, only to have this possibility tragically defeated. In this scene, just at the moment when a positive ending seems possible for Ruby, the audience realises that her search for happiness is now defeated.

Ruby's loss of sanity is depicted by her sudden shifts in character. She swings between meaningful questions such as 'what happened to me?' (p.31), her familiar child's scream of 'Where are you?'(p.30), and a complete introspection and rejection of her family in such muttered statements as 'Don't want no trouble' and 'Got enough to do' (p.31). These swings in Ruby's psychological and emotional states leave her father and sister nonplussed. The scene ends with them unable to communicate with Ruby, leaving the audience wondering if her institutional confinement will now last indefinitely.

Sandy revisits the children's home (pp.31–2)

The previous scenes have highlighted the extreme uncertainty and disorientation of Jimmy, Anne and Ruby, largely through their interactions with – or their inability to interact with – family members (especially mothers). In this scene, however, Sandy's disorientation is largely to do with place, rather than family. Sandy returns to the place of his childhood institutionalisation to find it radically changed. His disorientation is conveyed by his body language, in accordance with the stage direction '*a little lost*' (p.31). The offstage voice tells Sandy that the building is soon to be converted 'into luxury apartments' (p.31).

The 'riff-raff': a brief moment of humour

The irony of the conversion of the children's home into luxury apartments is not lost on Sandy. The offstage voice begins a kind of sales pitch, commenting on the 'Amazing space', and even putting a positive spin on the window bars that will 'keep out the riff-raff' (p.32). Sandy realises that Australia's white government and society would have regarded the Aboriginal children institutionalised here in the past as 'riff-raff'. That is, those who were kept inside in the past are now – because of social and economic disadvantage – kept firmly on the outside.

For Sandy, there would be little point in resisting economic or political forces at this point, and he continues on what seems to be an unending, life-long voyage with his suitcase, deciding he will 'best be moving ...' (p.32).

Racist insults (pp.32–4)

Key scene

In this intense, compact scene, issues such as racism, alcohol abuse, imprisonment, deaths in custody and the Stolen Generations are shown to be closely interrelated. Jimmy's life history shows that many of the significant problems experienced by Aboriginal people in the present may well have their origins in the past removal of children from their families.

Ignorance

Throughout the bar scene, *Stolen* makes the audience keenly aware of the reasons for Jimmy's drunkenness and hostility. However, there are no apparent reasons for the (unseen) white man's anger. Instead, white and black men strike out at each other with more or less equal ignorance of the other's perspective. This point is brought home when both characters say the word 'ignorant' simultaneously. The exchange of racist insults does nothing to alter their mutual ignorance or hostility.

Aboriginal deaths in custody

Jimmy ends his life by hanging himself in a prison cell. Notice how the bars of his bed double as prison bars. This meaning of the bars on the bed is established at the opening of the play: the stage direction indicates that 'JIMMY *gazes into the distance through the bars of his prison cell (his bed)*' (p.1). In this way, the link between the institutionalising of children and the high rates of imprisonment for Aboriginal people is strikingly and forcefully made.

White indifference

The cynical, indifferent attitude of white society – and especially of white authority figures – to the situation of Aboriginal people is summed up by the prison warden's remark. He implies that, even if Jimmy had been released from prison, he 'woulda been back here anyway' (p.34). Jimmy replies, as it were, from the dead, to stress the importance of maintaining hope for a possibly different future: 'Maybe, maybe not' (p.34).

Anne's scene (p.34)

Anne addresses the audience directly, no longer silenced and bewildered by the clamour of voices from her two families, but still quite uncertain about her own identity, about where she 'belongs'. She is caught between two worlds, which is one characteristic outcome of policies relating to the government project of assimilation. Anne challenges the audience, suggesting that broader social expectations, from 'blackfellas' as well as 'whitefellas', are also part of the dilemma for people who don't fall neatly into simplistically defined categories. Anne chooses to act pragmatically, deciding that she does not have to resolve all of her uncertainties in order to live her life: 'it's Mother's Day and I've got to make tracks', she declares. Her choice of gifts injects a note of humour into the scene: milk chocolates for her white mother and dark chocolates for her Aboriginal mother. The serious point Anne makes in this way is that the difference between these 'colours' is not, finally, all that important: what counts is the love she has for both her mothers.

Shirley's come full circle (p.35)

Shirley has the most unambiguously happy ending of any of the characters. Like Anne, Shirley directly addresses the audience, alone. Her identity is reaffirmed by her place within her family, rather than by any political action or a return to her place of birth. She has even moved from her home of eighteen years in order to be closer to her family. She does not identify herself – primarily – as an Aboriginal woman. Shirley's identity, as she seems to perceive it, is as a mother and grandmother.

Sandy at the end of the road (pp.35–6)

Sandy's reaction to a degree of personal independence, unlike Anne's and Shirley's, is to emphatically reclaim his identity as an Aboriginal person – rather than as a family member. Familial relations are less at stake for Sandy, perhaps because his family has become remote from his life due to his ceaseless moving.

The idea of 'home' is closely tied to Sandy's origins; place is as much a home as is family. It is also characterised in terms of a natural environment – a 'bit of red desert', a place to 'catch that fish!' (p.36) – rather than a built environment such as the children's home, or a road.

All the characters contribute to this final scene, as Sandy wanders over to each of them in turn. They indicate the place they feel they have reached in their lives after all that has happened. For Ruby and Jimmy these places are full of loss and sadness; for the others they are ambiguous, but they also hold undeniable hope for the future.

[Curtain call – p.36]

The actors are required to *'break out of their roles and talk in turn about their own experiences'* (p.36). This unconventional end to the play has the effect of showing that a relationship exists between the lives of the actors and the events they have been dramatising on the stage. Such a close connection is not normally presumed to exist: the conventional assumption is that the actors' skills will be sufficient to allow them to perform somebody else's experience – even if it is an entirely unfamiliar experience compared to their own – in a convincing, lifelike way on stage. In the case of *Stolen*'s unorthodox ending, there is no implied lessening of the actors' skills. However, the ways in which the policies and events relating to the Stolen Generations have impacted on the actors' *own* lives reinforce *Stolen*'s emphasis on the close relationship between representation and reality. This relationship is crucial if theatre is to have a strong sense of politics and to influence the politics of its audiences.

CHARACTERS & RELATIONSHIPS

Through its use of five contrasting characters, *Stolen* shows that the experience of being 'stolen' can take different forms and have widely varying effects on individuals.

Challenging the assumption of homogeneity

Stolen challenges the preconceived idea that all Aboriginal people are the same. Jane Harrison writes in her programme notes for the 1999 Melbourne season (reproduced at the end of the Currency edition of *Stolen*):

> My brief was to tell many stories, not just one, and not to represent Koories as homogeneous people who all think, feel and react the same way.[14]

This is an important statement, because some media representations can suggest that *all* members of the Stolen Generations came from the same circumstances, had the same experiences and reacted in the same ways. This is the assumption of a 'homogeneous people' that Harrison refers to, and it has two negative effects.

First, this assumption stereotypes Aboriginal people. Second, it implies that any evidence *differing* from the assumed circumstances and experiences of the Indigenous people concerned, places pressure on the legitimacy of the term 'Stolen Generations' – as if, for instance, the removal of Indigenous children from their families was not really a form of 'stealing'.

As *Stolen* persuasively demonstrates, however, a great deal *was* stolen from Aboriginal people through these government-sanctioned policies and practices.

---

14 Jane Harrison's 'Playwright's Note' is also included in the programme notes for the 1998 production, p.vii.

Stolen resists stereotyping the experience of being 'stolen' by showing its different forms, albeit with overlapping effects. The five characters are brought together in several scenes to show how their different situations share common aspects and problems. Additionally, each character is a complex individual, and each allows a number of important themes and issues to be represented and dramatised.

Jimmy

Key quotes

'Willy Wajurri and I've got a mother!' (p.27).

'I don't even know what having a mother feels like' (p.30).

'I'm going now, to be with my mother. I can't fight. I'm punched out' (p.34).

The transformation of Jimmy's personality

Jimmy's personality changes dramatically as he grows older, under the oppressive forces of white society, bureaucracy and law. This transformation is highlighted by the shifts in time that occur throughout *Stolen*. The best example is in the scene 'It rained the day' (pp.4–5), when Jimmy acts out a childhood incident in the family's chook yard. Then he shifts, for a moment, into his adult character, before waking as a child. Jimmy's past clearly haunts his adult life, and the disparity between his childhood and adult personalities – the former lively and laughing, the latter morose and silent – is illustrated dramatically in this scene. As the play unfolds, the reasons for this disparity become apparent.

The young Jimmy is bold and full of humour; he challenges authority, but without being destructive or malicious. As he grows older, the oppressiveness of white authority and, in particular, the disappointment of being denied contact with his mother (the one thing he continues to hope for while in the children's home) cause Jimmy's personality to alter.

The end of Jimmy's happiness and childhood innocence

Jimmy's innocence lasts longer than that of the other children, as shown by the scene 'Line-up 3', in which Jimmy alone is 'in the dark about what happens when the white family take home a child for the weekend' (p.20). When he is chosen he *'steps forward happily'* (p.21), but this marks the end of Jimmy's happiness. The immediate impact of his experience with the white family is staged in a later scene, 'Unspoken abuse 3' (p.23). He is seen *'holding a ball stiffly'* and *'can't answer for shame'*; the children realise that, like Ruby, he has 'promised not to tell' (p.23).

The more long-term effect of the abuse Jimmy experiences is dramatised in the scene 'Jimmy's being naughty again' (p.20), which immediately precedes 'Line-up 3'. Now an older boy, no longer in the children's home, Jimmy is a thief. This is an example of the sequence of scenes in *Stolen* not following chronological time, since the subsequent scenes, 'Line-up 3' and 'Unspoken abuse 3', return to Jimmy's childhood years in the home. Thus the audience sees the kind of person Jimmy becomes before seeing all of the factors that produce this person. His transformation from childhood happiness to a more adult rebelliousness and hostility is marked most clearly in 'Jimmy's being naughty again' by Jimmy's laughter, which is now 'more an angry laugh' (p.20).

There is a glimmer of hope when an Aboriginal man in a bar tells Jimmy his real name – Willy Wajurri – and that his mother is still alive. However, he becomes even more angry and hostile after his mother's death. The issues of racism, alcoholism, violence and Aboriginal deaths in custody are all touched on in the key scene 'Racist insults' (pp.32–4). The tragic end to Jimmy's life is seen to be an almost inevitable and understandable consequence of all that has happened to him.

Ruby

Key quotes

'I want my mummy ... Where are you?' (p.2).

'I promised not to tell' (p.8).

'Don't need no home of me own. Got enough to do' (pp.1, 35).

Ruby's character is the least developed, in the sense that she never enters the adult world of making choices and deciding what kind of a future she will have. Of course, in Jimmy's case that decision is finally a self-destructive one, but at least it is made in full consciousness of his situation in the world. Ruby and Jimmy are the two characters whose lives end up being destroyed largely as a result of their institutionalised childhoods. In contrast, Anne, Shirley and Sandy represent different kinds of futures for members of the Stolen Generations – futures that have a more positive, hopeful outlook, as well as difficulties and sadness.

Ruby's desire for nurturing

Ruby's desire for a nurturing environment is evident in her interaction with her doll ('Ruby's comforting her baby' pp.9–10). She calls the doll 'Ruby' and speaks as a mother, projecting onto the doll the care and love she herself longs for. Then she returns to her own identity, crying out 'Where are you?' in clear awareness of her own mother's absence. Ruby's deprivation of a loving, nurturing mother is reflected in the way she throws away her own doll in turn. The lack of a loving home life compounds the abuse she repeatedly receives on visits to the home of a white couple. Ruby's inability to speak about what has happened causes her to withdraw into herself, making it increasingly impossible for her to interact with others.

Ruby's real family

By the time Ruby's family re-establishes contact with her, she has retreated entirely into her own internal world. Even her sister's comforting words, 'we've come to take you home', take on threatening connotations to Ruby, so she draws back, saying 'Don't need no trouble' (p.31). For Ruby, 'home' means the children's home, which she has left behind: 'Don't live in no home anymore', she insists (p.31). This shows that it can sometimes be too late for even a loving home to make a difference for someone deprived of it for so many years.

Shirley

Key quotes

'After all these years to get used to it, it still hurts' (p.19).

'You people have been putting me on hold for twenty-seven years ...' (p.22).

'I have a daughter and a granddaughter – but more important – Tamara has a mother and a grandmother. And that's all that matters' (p.35).

Shirley represents the importance of family, and especially of motherhood, to identity and happiness. She is a strong, comforting presence in the children's home. Also, Shirley's experiences reflect the historical fact that the removal of children took place over more than one generation: what happens to Shirley as a child happens, in turn, to her own children.

Shirley's remnants of the past

All that is left to Shirley of her past are a few photographs ('Shirley's memories', p.17) and clothes – such as the *'tiny baby's jumper that she'd kept under her pillow'* (p.9). She has knitted many items of clothing for her children, without having had the opportunity to *'give them her symbols of love'* (p.19). These things link Shirley to her past, through memory and through her feelings of love for her family; they also represent her hope for the future, through the lives of her children.

Shirley's hope for the future

Despite her traumatic experiences, the loss of so much of her family life, and her pain and suffering that will never completely go away, Shirley is able to restore family ties. The relationship she re-establishes with her daughter Kate, and her new relationship with her granddaughter Tamara, enables a kind of release from the repetitions and enclosures of the past. This is represented by Shirley's decision to move from the house in which she has lived for eighteen years, in order 'to be closer to Kate and the baby' (p.35).

The birth of a new generation, and the hope that these family relationships will be allowed to continue and not be severed, emphasise the extent of what has been stolen from Aboriginal people. In the past, families were broken up, and each new generation was forced further and further away from traditional Indigenous cultures and knowledge. The promise of a new life, in a society that no longer quite so forcibly tries to assimilate and segregate Aboriginal people, is also the promise of a better future for all Aboriginal people. This promise for the future is signalled by Shirley standing *'in a beam of light at the front of the stage'* (p.35); the strong presence of light and Shirley's dominant position on the stage contrast strongly with the darkness and oppression so prevalent throughout the play.

Sandy

Key quotes

'Always on the run' (pp.3, 4).

'Do you wanna hear the story of the big bad Mungee? My grandfather told me this' (p.10).

'My people are from the desert. Home of the red sands' (p.22).

'Been everywhere. Except one place. Home' (p.35).

The most important person in Sandy's life is his mother. Sandy remembers her stories and her laughter; 'She was always laughing, my old mum' (p.22). Although Sandy no longer seems to have contact with his mother, or any of his family, after his time in the children's home, her presence in his past gives Sandy a strong sense of who he is, where he has come from, and – ultimately – a place to which he might one day be able to return.

Sandy 'always on the run'

As Sandy's name suggests, he is the character closest to a traditional understanding of Aboriginal identity. His name aligns him with a natural element – sand. Sandy's life is relatively nomadic, though not because he chooses to follow a traditional way of life but because social and material forces always work to unsettle him, to 'move him on'.

During his childhood Sandy is always trying to evade the Welfare. In the early scene, 'Hiding Sandy' (pp.3–4), Sandy's repeated phrase, 'Always on the run', establishes the pattern of flight and evasion that will characterise much of his future life. His circumstances, like those of the other characters, keep repeating themselves.

The Welfare's 'gift'

The Welfare finally catches up with Sandy, as he relates in 'A can of peas' (pp.19–20). The can of peas is part of the Welfare's token attempt to help poor Aboriginal families with food supplies. When the can is found at the back of a cupboard, past its use-by date, this insignificant, forgotten object is all it takes for the Welfare to destroy the family. The story makes it clear that the department's priority is not really to assist the family's wellbeing, as the name implies, but to find any reason, however spurious, to separate the family members from each other.

The continuation of storytelling and place

Sandy's character in *Stolen* represents the possibility of a future for traditional Aboriginal culture in which storytelling and place have central roles to play. Sandy leads both storytelling episodes, drawing the other children into playing the roles of mythical or spirit beings. He also seeks to return to the desert sands at the end of the play, representing the possibility of a return to one's place of origin – and the continued, central importance of place to Aboriginal identity and culture.

Anne

Key quotes

'My home's got lace curtains – and I've got a room of my own' (p.1).

'Life is full of tricky situations … to tan or not to tan' (p.16).

'I just thought it would be different, somehow' (p.28).

'What do I want? I don't know. I don't know where I belong anymore …' (p.34).

Anne represents some of the most characteristically dislocating effects of the assimilation policy on Aboriginal people (discussed further in 'Themes, ideas & values'). She is adopted into a comfortable home, in which material possessions (such as a doll and new pyjamas) are readily supplied. Her first line in *Stolen* draws attention to the material comfort – her own room, a home with 'lace curtains' (p.1) – that Anne, quite unlike the other children, can take for granted throughout most of her childhood. Nevertheless, Anne's relationship with her white parents is not a particularly close one, and they appear incapable of communicating directly and meaningfully with each other.

Anne's personal nightmare

In the scene 'The chosen' (p.7), Anne and her parents take turns to speak but at no stage do they directly address each other. This sense of speaking at cross-purposes, each alienated from the other, is reinforced in the later scene, 'Anne's told she's Aboriginal' (pp.13–14). Anne is shocked on receiving this information – 'This is a nightmare!' she exclaims (p.14) – but the shock is caused not by her birth mother's (and therefore her own) Aboriginality but by her white parents' deception and 'shame'. It is the betrayal of trust that this scene represents as being most hurtful.

The scenes in which Anne lives with her white parents are alternated with scenes in which she is still in the Cranby Children's Home. This is another example of Harrison's flexibility with time. Anne does not simply progress smoothly from one environment to the next, but each life stage and experience informs and affects the others, past and future, in some way.

In-between black and white

Anne's desire to know her Aboriginal family causes her to be caught in-between the two families and their cultures. She retains features of white culture and identity, in accordance with how she has been brought up by her white parents, but she also partly identifies as Aboriginal. The desire to maintain kinship links is a significant part of Anne's choice to acknowledge her Aboriginality.

In the scene 'Am I black or white?' (pp.28–9) Anne initially is claimed by both her families, then rejected by both. The white parents see Anne's interest in her Aboriginal family in terms of a betrayal of all they have given her; they are increasingly resentful and hostile, challenging Anne for explanations and reasons when she is unable to articulate them. The black voices also become increasingly threatening and antagonistic, showing how difficult it could be for someone like Anne to be accepted by an Indigenous community after being outside it for so many years.

Anne later turns this sense of confusion and alienation back onto the audience, directly addressing its 'blackfellas' and 'whitefellas' near the play's end ('Anne's scene', p.34). This prevents her sense of confusion and alienation turning into a completely personal problem, and makes it clear that it results from, and is characteristic of, broader social attitudes and prejudices – in which the audience, too, is complicit.

Relationships with mothers

Key quotes

RUBY: 'Where are you?' (pp.2, 10, 25, 31).

JIMMY: 'When's my mum gunna come for me?' (p.16).

SANDY: 'My mother, she loved me, but she called me Sandy anyway. She sure had a sense of humour that one' (p.23).

JIMMY: 'They kept saying she was dead … but I could feel her spirit' (p.33).

ANNE: 'Either way, I love them both' (pp.34, 36).

The strongest emotional bonds in *Stolen* are those between Aboriginal mothers and children. In particular, these relationships include Shirley and her daughter Kate, and Jimmy and his mother Nancy Wajurri. Sandy and Ruby also experience very strong feelings of loss due to the absence of their mothers in their lives.

Sandy's bond with his mother is bound up with a strong connection to place, 'that bit of red desert' (p.36). On the other hand, Ruby's bond with her mother is through a close, nurturing relationship very early in her life, a relationship that can never be restored or replaced. Thus Sandy is finally able to return home – to the place, if not necessarily to his mother – whereas Ruby can only repeat tragically her claim that she doesn't 'need no home of me own' (p.35).

Jimmy and Anne: two different searches for mothers

Both Jimmy and Anne search for their mothers in *Stolen*, but in different fashions. Jimmy desperately wants to be with his mother again, although he is told throughout his time in the Cranby Children's Home that she is dead. Anne's knowledge of her birth-mother is virtually nonexistent until her white mother informs her that she is still alive – yet Anne is ambivalent about how close she will become, or wants to become, to her Aboriginal mother.

Jimmy's identity is affirmed – and, in a sense, returned to him – when an Aboriginal man tells him that not only is Nancy still alive, but that Jimmy's name is actually Willy Wajurri. Jimmy gains reassurance and a sense of direction from this knowledge. This contrasts with Anne's situation, since meeting her Aboriginal family makes her own identity *more* fraught and confused. When the two families' combined voices demand 'Who do you think you are?'(p.29), Anne has no way of answering, even to herself.

Interestingly, in 'Anne's scene', Anne ties her decision to identify, at least partly, as Aboriginal, to her relationship with her Aboriginal mother. She says nothing, in contrast, about her relationships with either of her fathers. This reinforces *Stolen*'s representation of the forced removal of Indigenous children from their families as impacting much more on *mother*–child relations than on *father*–child relations. It could be argued that the play's politics are partly feminist in their engagement with Aboriginal issues.

Mother–child relationships: described rather than enacted

Stolen narrates most of the circumstances of its characters' relationships, rather than dramatising them. That is, the play represents the relationships in terms of the enforced separations between mothers and children (along with the longings on both sides) – rather than the interactions between them. To some degree this is a limitation that derives from the decision to only have five actors. However, the characterisation of these relationships in terms of *distance* and *separation* rather than *closeness* and *intimacy* makes an important thematic point about the effects of the assimilation and separation policies.

Relationships with non-Aboriginal people

The relationships between Aboriginal and non-Aboriginal characters in *Stolen* are fraught and adversarial. Even the loving relationship between Anne and her white parents is characterised by emotional distance and misunderstandings. The absence of white actors and characters on the actual stage emphasises the radically different experiences and histories of black and white cultures throughout most of the twentieth century.

White Australians; 'whitening' of Indigenous characters

A number of offstage voices feature in *Stolen*, most of them representing white individuals. The white characters exercising power over the children's lives remain shadowy, often in a literal sense. In the scene 'Line-up 1' (p.6), the white couple is absent; the idea of whiteness is present in the form of a white spotlight that picks out Ruby, and *'in the bright light she looks white'* (p.6). In the following scene, Anne's parents are represented by *'shadows falling on to a Venetian blind or a white sheet'* (p.6). A white spotlight on Anne effects an unsettling reversal: Anne is whitened, and the (white) parents appear dark.

The fact that white characters are out of sight allows Aboriginal people to be in the foreground, and also reflects the remote, faceless aspects of white power in relation to Aboriginal lives. Under these conditions, any meaningful dialogue between black and white people is impossible; there are no mechanisms available to the Aboriginal characters for negotiating better circumstances.

THEMES, IDEAS & VALUES

Home

Key quotes

JIMMY: 'I wanna go home' (p.15).

RUBY: 'Don't need no home of me own. I've got enough to do' (pp.1, 35).

SANDY: 'Been everywhere. Except one place. Home' (p.35).

The setting for most of *Stolen* is the Cranby Children's Home, in which the children are resident during the 1950s and 1960s. This time frame is established by Nancy Wajurri's letters to Jimmy, and by Sandy's story of his life after leaving the home in 'Sandy's life on the road' (pp.25–6).

The children think of their *real* home, though, as being somewhere else. In 'Line-up 1', the prospect of a weekend visit leads Sandy to ask, hopefully, 'Back home ...?' but Shirley makes it clear: 'Not our homes, Sandy, *their* home' (p.6). The ideas of 'home' and 'family' are closely intertwined, and for the children they always seem out of reach, something that other people have but the children do not, and will not, have.

The emphasis on home in the opening

The central issue of home is established in the opening lines of *Stolen*'s second scene, 'Arriving'. The first three characters to speak each say 'home' in their first sentence – and each has a completely different attitude towards, and relationship with, 'home'.

Ruby's sense of home

Ruby declares that she doesn't need 'no home of me own' (p.1). At first this may look like a determined streak of independence, but as the play unfolds it becomes clear that Ruby needed a home of her own more than anything else. By the end of the play, it is too late even for a home to make things right for Ruby, and when she repeats the exact words with which she begins 'Adult flashes' in 'Sandy at the end of the road' (p.35), her statement about not needing a home takes on tragic overtones.

Anne's sense of home

Unlike the other characters, Anne does experience a safe, comfortable home in her childhood, one that brings a great deal of pleasure. Her problems are much more to do with identity. Nevertheless, Anne's sense of where she belongs is completely changed when she learns that her mother is Aboriginal, reinforcing the interconnectedness of home, kinship and family.

Shirley's sense of home

Shirley also emphasises the link between home and family. In 'Shirley's come full circle' (p.35), she says 'home is where the heart is', drawing on a cliché in order to make the distinction between a particular location and a feeling. The implication is that the house in which she lived 'for eighteen years' is less a home than a place 'closer to Kate and the baby'.

Sandy's sense of home at the end of the road

Sandy begins *Stolen* by saying that he carries his home with him – like Ruby, suggesting that he is independent of other people or any single, particular place. However, like Ruby, the meaning of Sandy's words is transformed by his experiences, and by the audience's experience of watching the play. In the final scene, in 'Sandy at the end of the road', Sandy no longer thinks that home is completely transportable, but that it *is* a particular place – the place he was born. The positive outlook at the end of *Stolen* is largely generated by the way in which it holds open the promise of Sandy's return to this place.

The 'end of the road' carries a double meaning. One meaning is negative: it signals frustration and the lack of options for the future facing Aboriginal people whose lives have been destroyed by racist government policies and actions. But the other meaning is positive. Roads allow colonial populations to possess and control territory; so they are inextricably associated with the dominant white culture and government of Australia. Therefore, Sandy's decision to be at the 'end' of the road shows his determination to no longer follow the path mapped out for him by white society. As he says, 'I don't have to run anymore' (p.36). Instead, he will return to his own country and to Aboriginal ways of knowing where 'home' is.

Family

Key quotes

SHIRLEY: 'I have a daughter and a granddaughter … that's all that matters' (p.35).

JIMMY: 'I don't even know what having a mother feels like' (p.30).

Like the issue of home, the issue of family is one to which the children attach great importance, even though their experiences of being in a stable, loving family are minimal. The children's sense of belonging to a family, then, is maintained through memory and desire. The children yearn for the family they remember and imagine to be still intact; above all, they long for their mothers. Ruby's longing for her mother is shown by her cry, recurring throughout *Stolen*, 'Where are you?' (pp.2,10). In Shirley's case, since the play shows her more often as an adult than as a child, her strongest desire is to be with her own children. Relationships between mothers and children – and their absence – are discussed in 'Characters & relationships'. Family is very closely associated with the characters' sense of identity.

Identity

Key quotes

JIMMY: 'Willy Wajurri and I've got a mother!' (p.27).

VOICES: 'Who do you think you are?' (p.29).

When Aboriginal children were placed in institutions, identity was stifled by a system that denied them any contact with their culture. The first task for the missionaries was to change the children's Aboriginal identity. Koorie writer John Moriarty remembers their message like this:

> [they would say] we must forsake our 'heathen' background. All those learnings that you had, you must forget all about them. You must not have your Aboriginal names, you must not have any of the languages.[15]

In spite of all the official attempts to destroy children's knowledge of Aboriginal culture – to stop their use of Aboriginal languages, change their names and control their every movement, often through deception and lies – the children managed to keep alive the spark of identity, longing to return to their families and cultures.

The Australian government's definition of Aboriginality for the purposes of policy and administration is:

> An Aboriginal or Torres Strait Islander is a person of Aboriginal or Torres Strait Islander descent, who identifies with and is accepted as such by the community with which he or she is associated.

In *Stolen*, though, identity – especially Aboriginal identity – means something slightly different for each character. For Shirley, identity is mostly defined by family; as she says of being a mother and grandmother, 'that's all that matters' (p.35). Jimmy's identity is also related to kinship. His relationship to his mother is what enables him to be identified by an Aboriginal man as 'one of Nancy's boys' (p.27). Jimmy thus reclaims knowledge of his own name and identity: 'Willy Wajurri and I've got a mother!' (p.27).

For Sandy, though, family seems remote; his identity is more to do with his Aboriginality, and with being from a particular place: 'My people are from the desert' (p.22). Like Jimmy, Sandy's identity, in terms of his family *and* in terms of his place of origin, is strongly related to memories of his mother.

Anne's identity is questioned by both her black and white families: 'Who do you think you are?' they ask (p.29). She finds it impossible to

---

15 John Moriarty, *Saltwater Fella*, Penguin, Victoria, 2000, p.23.

answer this question simply, and she admits: 'I don't know where I belong anymore' (p.34). In order to get on with her life ('I've got to make tracks', p.34), Anne tries to keep the best features from both aspects of her upbringing and ancestry. For Anne this means loving both her mothers.

Identity, race and 'colour'

Anne's anxiety about her skin colour ('To tan or not to tan?') highlights the inherently contradictory qualities of identity and race. The issue (and desirability) of 'tanning' indicates how superficial, on one level, the question of skin colour is, since it can be altered merely by lying in the sun. On another level, though, skin colour is extremely significant in a society that places so much importance on race. Skin colour is the most visible marker of race; that is, it signifies a difference on the body's surface that is read as being more than skin deep.

The significance of skin colour is also evident in the line-up sequence ('Line-up 1', p.6). In this scene, the stage direction indicates the children should line up twice, the second time in an order determined by their skin colour. This draws the audience's attention to skin colour as a criterion for the children's selection, and also signals that the children themselves are conscious of its importance.

The assimilation policy

Key quotes

MOTHER: 'We've given you everything – a home, an education, a future' (p.28).

ANNE: 'I don't know where I belong anymore ...' (p.34).

The assimilation policy was closely tied to the removal of children from Aboriginal families throughout much of the twentieth century. The policies of assimilation and segregation systematically eroded the cultural, physical, social and emotional fabric of Indigenous society.

The children's confusion about their identities, the loss of their families and homes, and the limited life options available to them are aspects of the devastating impact of the assimilation policy. Notice, then, the profound irony of the assimilation policy's 'promise' – represented in *Stolen* by what Anne's white parents claim they have given her – to provide a 'future' to Aboriginal people. Far from being a gift from white people, a future for Aboriginal people is precisely what has been most threatened as a result of the treatment they have received from white government and society in Australia.

In between black and white

Having an identity that is in between black and white is a characteristic effect of the assimilation policy on individuals. In *Stolen* this effect is most clearly evident in the character of Anne. In contrast, Jimmy and Sandy locate themselves in defiant opposition to white society, though as isolated individuals, since they are not represented as strongly within any Aboriginal community.

It is worth noting the pun on 'coconut' in one scene that particularly highlights Anne's uncertainty about her identity: 'To tan or not to tan?' Coconut oil is what Anne applies to her skin in order to acquire a tan. The term 'coconut' also carries the slang meaning of 'black on the outside, white on the inside', referring to a black person who behaves like a white person. It is a derogatory term in the sense that it implies that the person has in some way betrayed their 'real' identity or heritage. Anne's character suggests that identity is far more complex than this – that there is no real or underlying identity that is unambiguously 'black' or 'white'. One's 'internal' sense of identity can change through life experiences, and can be, at any time, quite confused and undecided.

Working identities

In *Stolen*, the roles available to the children once they leave the home fail to fulfil the assimilation policy's promise of inclusion. They will participate in white society only by taking on the most menial, working-class occupations: cooks, cleaners and so on. In the scene 'Cleaning routine 2' the children parody the game, 'what are you going to be when you grow up?', to the tune of 'We're Happy Little Vegemites' (p.18). This routine has the double function of mocking the assimilation policy and of showing the children to be entirely aware of how social forces are working against them. The children will be 'assimilated' within white society only to the extent that they can be exploited.

Racism

Key quotes

VOICE: 'Who's back there? ... You black bastards! I'll call the cops' (p.20).

VOICE: 'Hey, boong, go back to the desert where you belong ...' (p.33).

JIMMY: 'I've been a thug and a thief – but I've never stolen anyone's soul ...' (p.34).

WARDEN: 'The bastard woulda been back here anyway' (p.34).

Many of the Stolen Generations – not to mention Aboriginal people more generally – suffered from various forms of racism, leading to severe depression and social problems. Some saw suicide as their only option in order to end the pain and suffering. Jimmy's experiences in *Stolen* show how events could overtake somebody's life and character in this way. The HREOC report, *Bringing Them Home,* states:

> by the early 1950s, the international prohibition of racial discrimination of the kind to which indigenous families and children were subjected was well recognised, even in Australia.[16]

Of course, 'recognition' is one thing, but progressive actions are another thing entirely. Despite *Stolen*'s fluid, imprecise time frame, enough dates are given to locate most of the play's action in the post-war period – the 1950s and 1960s, exactly the period when 'international prohibition of racial discrimination was ... recognised'.

Deaths in custody

The cumulative effect of Jimmy's institutionalisation, the lies he has been told about his mother, her death shortly before he was able to meet her,

16 HREOC, *Bringing Them Home*, p.27.

and the violence and racism he experiences in society is that Jimmy gives up all hope for his future. He hangs himself in his prison cell, raising the very important issue of Aboriginal deaths in custody.

Although a Royal Commission into Aboriginal deaths in Custody was completed in 1990, the Commission's recommendations have not been acted upon to any significant degree. The rates of imprisonment of Aboriginal people, and of Aboriginal deaths in custody, remain as high as when the Royal Commission took place, if not higher.

In *Stolen*, this issue is represented from an Aboriginal perspective – not as a mere statistic, but as the end result of complex forces and in terms of a unique, individual life that found those forces finally overwhelming. The reasons for Jimmy's suicide are dramatically rendered. Although the audience is certainly able to understand this scene in terms of a personal tragedy, it is also able to see the implication of broader social and material factors in Jimmy's decision to end his life.

Sexual, physical and emotional abuse

Key quotes

CHILDREN: 'He gave her a doll. What else did ya do?'

RUBY: 'I promised not to tell' (p.8).

The experience of various forms of abuse by children placed in institutions of foster homes was not uncommon. *Bringing Them Home* states that: 'one in six children who were institutionalised reported physical assault and punishment'.[17] John Moriarty had this experience of being institutionalised as a child:

> If you got caught doing things wrong, we were belted. Usually it was a leather strap across the backside. On April Fools' Day, I got up and was really looking forward to my birthday, but first thing I got belted, I don't know what I did wrong.[18]

17 HREOC, *Bringing Them Home*, p.16.

18 John Moriarty, *Saltwater Fella*, p.38.

Welfare officers failed to protect Indigenous children from these abuses. One in ten of those who were removed from their families as children allege that they were sexually abused in a work placement organised by the Protection Board or institution. One testimonial included in *Bringing Them Home* shows how difficult it was for the children to speak up:

> Our foster mother insisted that she had to be in the room when the Welfare officer visited ... so we never had a chance to complain ... Welfare never gave us a chance.[19]

In *Stolen*, both Ruby and Jimmy suffer implied sexual abuse at the hands of a white man, and are made to promise that they will not tell anyone about what happened. The gifts they receive – a doll (p.8) and a 'pitcha book' (p.15) for Ruby; a ball for Jimmy (p.23) – are not really gifts, but means of purchasing the children's silence. This allows the perpetrator to avoid being charged, so that the offences are repeated.

Physical abuse is represented in *Stolen* in the children's lives once they have left the children's home – though, as John Moriarty's anecdote indicates, violence was also experienced inside institutions. Ruby is beaten by several figures at the opening of 'Ruby's descent into madness' (pp.24, 25), though the message of this scene is that the real damage done to her is not so much physical as mental.

Jimmy fights a white man in 'Racist insults'; but again, the damage is less physical than emotional. Jimmy's violence leads to his imprisonment, which – as his letter shows – is what really defeats him: 'ya spirit just shrivels up inside' (p.34).

19 HREOC, *Bringing Them Home*, p.17.

Ignorance, denial and deception

Key quotes

RUBY: 'I promised not to tell' (pp.8, 15).

ANNE: 'I want to know why you didn't tell me about this before' (p.14).

SHIRLEY: 'You people have been putting me on hold for twenty-seven years …' (p.22).

The five characters are caught up in a network of subterfuge and deception. They lack any power to act, or even speak, against the system. In turn, the system denies them knowledge of, or contact with, their Aboriginal families or culture. Ruby's admission that she 'promised not to tell' (pp.8,15) represents the silencing of Aboriginal children about what was happening to them, and it reflects how they were trapped into going along with the system that abused and exploited them.

Official denials about the Stolen Generations did not end with the closure of the children's homes, but continue in various guises in the present (see 'Background & context') to the detriment of Aboriginal people and of Australian society as a whole.

Bringing Them Home includes testimonies that show how pervasive and effective the practices of lying and deceiving were in destroying links between Aboriginal children and the families from which they had been taken. Many children were told their families did not want them, or were dead. One testimonial recalls, 'we were told that our mother was an alcoholic and that she was a prostitute and she didn't care about us'.[20] Another relates an incredible, devastating discovery:

> One of the girls was doing Matron's office, and there was all these letters that the girls had written back to parents and family – the answers were all in the garbage bin … that was one way they stopped us keeping in contact with our families.[21]

---

20 HREOC, *Bringing Them Home*, p.15.
21 HREOC, *Bringing Them Home*, p.14.

These experiences are reflected in *Stolen* by Jimmy's inability to communicate directly with his mother due to the administration's policy to prevent it; the audience hears their voices, but they are deaf to each other:

> JIMMY: When's my mum gunna come for me?
> JIMMY'S MOTHER: We haven't had any replies from all our letters.
> VOICE: Your mother's not coming. She's dead. (p.16)

And Shirley's retort that 'You people have been putting me on hold for twenty-seven years' (p.22) shows how powerful bureaucratic systems are able to defer any admission of the true state of affairs if it suits them – as easily as putting somebody on hold on the phone.

The filing cabinet

The slamming shut of the filing cabinet door is a dramatic metaphor for the silencing and deferral practised by government and bureaucracy. The filing cabinet encloses Nancy Wajurri's letters to Jimmy in order to perpetuate the lies of white officials. Jimmy has absolutely no way of accessing the letters and confronting the matron with her deception and cruelty.

When Sandy returns to (what had been) the Cranby Children's Home, he finds it being converted into luxury apartments (pp.31–2). Nobody prevents him from looking inside the filing cabinet – it is completely empty. All the official records of the children's lives have, it seems, been placed somewhere else (equally unobtainable) or destroyed. It is as if the children were never there – a form of erasure of history.

The denial of Aboriginal identity

In 'Anne's told she's Aboriginal', lying just below the surface of the parents' insistence that they want only the 'best' for Anne is the idea that what is best is a complete denial of her Aboriginality. They seem to believe they are reassuring her when they say: 'No-one need ever know' (p.14). Of course, Anne has no way of judging whether denial of her Aboriginality is a good thing, largely because it *has* remained unspoken, and the racist ideology that underpins it has also been kept hidden.

When the identity of her mother is revealed to her, Anne is left alone to try to make sense of it, as her white parents walk off to comfort each other. Feelings of alienation and bewilderment are common to all the characters in *Stolen*, and are largely generated by white denial, ignorance and racism.

A gift for Sandy

When Sandy relates his life story to a woman – presumably a white woman – at a bus stop, she seems to have no means of responding in any meaningful way. Her gift of twenty dollars is rewarded with an 'amused' look from Sandy (p.26); it seems kindly meant, but it is an utterly inadequate form of compensation.

The woman cannot relate to Sandy's life, so she acknowledges him in terms that are meaningful and significant to her – through a small gift of money. Although not altogether without value, this gift represents a form of ignorance on her part, since it cannot replace or even help restore what has been taken away from Sandy: his family, and his home.

Storytelling, survival and hope

Key quotes

SANDY: 'When I was a little boy, my mother would tell me the story of how the desert sands were created, a long time ago' (p.22).

JIMMY: 'Brothers, don't give up fighting' (p.34).

SANDY: 'Been everywhere. Except one place … I'm going back … Back to me place. That bit of red desert. I still remember it. The sand must have seeped into me brain' (pp.35–6).

ANNE: 'I don't know where I belong anymore … But hey, it's Mother's Day … I got Mum some milk chocolates. And I got my *mother* some dark chocolates … Either way, I love them both' (p.34)

In a number of ways, *Stolen* balances its representations of trauma, abuse, suffering and persecution with more positive, optimistic attitudes. Different forms of survival are seen to be possible. Even Jimmy, who stops fighting, expresses hope that others will continue to 'fight' in order to prevent the past repeating itself in the future. Sandy, Shirley and Anne, however, do not see their own futures in terms of a fight; they are more focused on what sources of meaning are available to them personally – meanings that are, in each case, couched in terms of a relationship.

The desire to be reunited with family keeps alive a glimmer of hope for the children. Jimmy's hope that he will be reunited with his mother sustains him for a long time, despite the lies and abuse to which he is subjected. For Shirley, her relationships with her daughter and granddaughter are 'all that matters' (p.35) – her joy in 'Shirley's come full circle' (p.35) is as moving as any of the earlier scenes of pain and unhappiness.

Anne is finally reunited with her Aboriginal mother and she also maintains a loving relationship with her white mother. The difficulties of her situation are not completely resolved – as she says, 'I don't know where I belong anymore' (p.34) – but she finds a way of moving on and looking ahead.

Sandy's sense of optimism has to do with a relationship to place, rather than to family. The place he is from is what, for Sandy, promises a form of belonging – of course, it is also tied to his memories of his mother. Sandy's ability to survive is also linked with the value he places on storytelling as a form of cultural memory, and as a source of community.

When Sandy tells the story of the Mungee to the other children, it is a way of remembering a part of his culture, a story that has been told to him by his grandfather – emphasising the link between Aboriginal culture and family. It begins to take the form of an imaginative escape from the restrictions and prohibitions of the children's home. As the story unfolds, however, its close relationship to the children's present situation becomes all too clear. That is, the story is not so much an escape from the children's institutionalisation as a critical comment on it.

Similarly, it is possible to see *Stolen* (as a piece of theatre) not as an escape from reality but as a critical comment on Australia's contemporary situation with respect to its Indigenous people. It also sends a positive message to Indigenous audiences and communities about the stories of hope that can, and must, continue to be told.

QUESTIONS & ANSWERS

This section focuses on your analytical writing on the text, and gives you strategies for producing high-quality responses in your coursework and exam essays.

Essay writing – an overview

An essay on a literary work is a formal and serious piece of writing that presents your point of view on the text, usually in response to a given topic. Your 'point of view' in an essay is your interpretation of the meaning of the text's language, structure, characters, situations and events, supported by detailed analysis of textual evidence.

Analyse – don't summarise

In your essays it is important to avoid simply summarising what happens in a text.

- A **summary** is a description or paraphrase (retelling in different words) of the characters and events. For example: 'Macbeth has a horrifying vision of a dagger dripping with blood before he goes to murder King Duncan.'
- An **analysis** is an explanation of the real meaning or significance that lies 'beneath' the text's words (and images, for a film). For example: 'Macbeth's vision of a bloody dagger shows how deeply uneasy he is about the violent act he is contemplating, and conveys his sense that supernatural forces are impelling him to act.'

A limited amount of summary is sometimes necessary to let your reader know which part of the text you wish to discuss. However, always keep this to a minimum and follow it immediately with your analysis of what this part of the text is really telling us.

Plan your essay

Carefully plan your essay so that you have a clear idea of what you are going to say. The plan ensures that your ideas flow logically, that your argument remains consistent and that you stay on the topic. An essay plan should be a list of **brief dot points** – no more than half a page.

Include your central argument or main contention – a concise statement (usually in a single sentence) of your overall response to the topic. See 'Analysing a Sample Topic' for guidelines on how to formulate a main contention.

Write three or four dot points for each paragraph, indicating the main idea and evidence/examples from the text. Note that in your essay you will need to *expand* on these points and *analyse* the evidence.

Structure your essay

An essay is a complete, self-contained piece of writing. It has a clear beginning (the introduction), middle (several body paragraphs) and end (the last paragraph or conclusion). It must also have a central argument that runs throughout, linking each paragraph to form a coherent whole. See examples of introductions and conclusions in the 'Analysing a Sample Topic' and 'Sample Answer' sections.

The introduction establishes your overall response to the topic. It includes your main contention and outlines the main evidence you will refer to in the course of the essay. Write your introduction *after* you have done a plan and *before* you write the rest of the essay.

The body paragraphs argue your case – they present evidence from the text and explain how this evidence supports your argument. Each body paragraph needs:

- a strong **topic sentence** (usually the first sentence) that states the main point being made in the paragraph
- **evidence** from the text, including some brief quotations
- **analysis** of the textual evidence, with explanation of its significance and how it supports your argument
- **links back to the topic** in one or more statements, usually towards the end of the paragraph.

Connect the body paragraphs so that your discussion flows smoothly. Use some linking words and phrases such as 'similarly' and 'on the other hand', though don't start every paragraph like this. Another strategy is to use a significant word from the last sentence of one paragraph in the first sentence of the next.

Use key terms from the topic – or synonyms for them – throughout, so the relevance of your discussion to the topic is always clear.

The conclusion ties everything together and finishes the essay. It includes strong statements that emphasise your central argument and provide a clear response to the topic.

Avoid simply restating the points made earlier in the essay – this will end on a very flat note and imply that you have run out of ideas and vocabulary. The conclusion should be a logical extension of what you have written, not just a repetition or summary of it. Writing an effective conclusion can be a challenge. Try using these tips:

- Start by linking back to the final sentence of the second-last paragraph – this helps your writing to flow, rather than leaping back to your main contention straight away.
- Use synonyms and expressions with equivalent meanings to vary your vocabulary. This allows you to reinforce your line of argument without being repetitive.
- When planning your essay, think of one or two broad statements or observations about the text's wider meaning. These should be related to the topic and your overall argument. Keep them for the conclusion, since they will give you something 'new' to say but still follow logically from your discussion. The introduction will be focused on the topic, but the conclusion can present a wider view of the text.

Essay topics

1 "She sure had a sense of humour that one." 'In *Stolen*, the characters' ability to find glimpses of humour in tragic, hopeless situations is a key aspect of their survival and their capacity to invest their lives with meaning.' Discuss.

2 "Maybe we'll be like strangers." Discuss the ways in which *Stolen* shows how government policies and practices caused Indigenous children and their families to become alienated from each other.

3 "This is a nightmare!" 'The most nightmarish aspects of *Stolen* are the ways in which the children lose control over their own lives.' Discuss.

4 Examine how Jane Harrison uses stage directions and 'special effects' (lighting, sounds, smells and so on) to represent the children's feelings and their circumstances of being stolen.

5 Discuss how the lack of an obvious chronological order in the play generates both a sense of dislocation and a sense of how past events determine present circumstances.

6 "Maybe we'll be like strangers." Discuss the ways in which *Stolen* shows how government policies and practices caused Indigenous children and their families to become alienated from each other.

7 "I wanna go home." 'In *Stolen*, as for actual members of the Stolen Generations, what is really stolen from the children is any chance of having a home.' Discuss.

8 "I don't know where I belong anymore." Discuss the ways in which *Stolen* shows how members of the Stolen Generations have been dispossessed not just of their families but also of a place to which they belong.

9 "I promised not to tell." '*Stolen* shows that various forms of denial are a major source of pain and suffering for the Stolen Generations.' Discuss.

10 "And the people would never forget." How does *Stolen* show that the effects of the removal of Aboriginal children from their families are ongoing, remaining with them for life?

Analysing a sample topic

"Maybe we'll be like strangers". Discuss the ways in which *Stolen* shows how government policies and practices caused Indigenous children and their families to become alienated from each other.

First, consider what the topic implies – that *Stolen*'s characters and their families become alienated from each other. Think about questioning that assertion in order to establish to what extent you agree with it. Do the Aboriginal characters really become strangers to each other and their families? Or do they find ways of transcending the government's interventions in their lives?

The key words are 'strangers', 'alienated', 'children' and 'families'. The topic's central issue is how *Stolen* shows relationships between Aboriginal people, and especially kinship ties, to be broken down, so that even family members become 'strangers' to each other.

The context for the quotation is Nancy Wajurri's question as she waits, after twenty-six years, to meet her son. She is hopeful, but the events of her life have also made her full of doubts. This uncertainty is never resolved, because Nancy Wajurri dies before the meeting can take place. The play strongly suggests that Nancy and Jimmy *would* have re-established a lasting and meaningful relationship if they had had the opportunity, despite many years of separation.

Your response and argument will depend on the extent of your agreement with the topic's assertion. It is possible that you will agree completely; in that case, you must produce evidence showing the wide-ranging ways in which Aboriginal people become alienated from each other and from their families in *Stolen*. Or, you may take the opposite point of view: that these characters always remain close to each other in an emotional sense, even if they are 'separated', and kinship ties can transcend even the separation of death.

Perhaps the most interesting answer lies somewhere in-between: there are forces in *Stolen* that dislocate the relationships between Aboriginal people and, especially, between family members; but in some cases these forces are resisted, and relationships survive.

Examples of Aboriginal people becoming strangers to each other include:

- The removal of children from their families produces feelings of alienation. The primary relationship that suffers is between child and mother: Shirley and her son; Jimmy and his mother; Anne and her Aboriginal mother, and later her adoptive mother too.
- Ruby's breakdown is largely a result of abuse. She is beaten in the scene 'Ruby's Descent into Madness'. But the nature of another part of the abuse she receives is never made explicit because Ruby is forbidden to say what it is – but the audience is most likely to conclude that it is sexual. Ruby's inability to speak about it increases her isolation from the children. Finally she withdraws so far into herself that she is unable even to recognise her family: 'Who are you?' she asks them.
- As *Stolen* proceeds, the children are increasingly isolated from each other and from their families and communities as they set out on their own lives: Sandy moves from place to place on his own; Jimmy hangs himself in despair; Ruby is unable to communicate with anyone.

There are also examples that show how relationships can survive the alienating effects of government policy and social prejudice. You might consider the following:

- The children band together in various activities, such as the cleaning routines, or participate in 'Sandy's story of the Mungee' (pp.10–11) and 'Desert sands' (p.22) by acting out aspects of the narratives.
- Jimmy and his mother long to communicate and to be reunited for twenty-six years, despite the forces keeping them separated.

- Anne meets her Aboriginal mother and 'thought it would be different somehow' (p.28). This indicates how far she has moved from her Aboriginal family and culture, but nevertheless she wants to maintain a close connection with both mothers – 'I love them both' (p.34). Rather than become alienated from her white and black families, she decides to keep and develop the emotional bonds she has with both.
- Shirley is no stranger to her daughter, despite her years of separation. At the play's end they are reunited and Shirley has even gained a granddaughter.

In the conclusion to your essay, bring together the various strands of argument – the different aspects of alienation, as well as (if you choose to highlight them) the aspects that prevent Aboriginal people from becoming complete strangers to one another. Restate your main contention or argument in terms of a precise, coherent response to the topic.

SAMPLE ANSWER

'*Stolen* shows how a sense of identity, and belonging to a family, are fundamentally interconnected.' Discuss.

One of *Stolen*'s strongest ideas is that, when Aboriginal children were removed from their families, many interconnected attributes and qualities were also stolen, with effects lasting for entire lifetimes. Children were not only dispossessed of their families, but also of their sense of identity. *Stolen* shows that it is impossible simply to impose a new identity on a young child through the replacement of a family home with an institutional 'home'. Rather, belonging to a family is the way in which identity is acquired and sustained, not only early in life but throughout it.

Jimmy's long search for his mother is perhaps the clearest example of the interconnectedness of identity and family since, at the moment when he learns his mother is still alive, he also recovers his true name. The substitution of names was one way in which institutions attempted to foster a new, 'white' identity for Aboriginal children and to smoothly assimilate them into white society. Of course, to some extent these names and identities stuck, as shown by Jimmy's initial reaction of disbelief and denial: 'my name's not Willy and she's not my mother'. However, the truth of what Jimmy is told sinks in and his anger gives way to laughter and hope. Jimmy realises how closely his renewed sense of self is connected to his rediscovery of the people to whom he belongs: 'Willy Wajurri and I've got a mother'.

Sandy's sense of identity is also intimately connected to his affection for his mother. Unlike Jimmy, though, Sandy seems to have no expectation that he will see his mother again. His identity comes largely from his understanding of where he is from, his family's place: 'my people are from the desert'. Through Sandy, the play suggests that, for Aboriginal people, belonging to a family also means belonging to a place. Despite Sandy's many years of being 'on the move', he retains a kind of familiarity with his place of origin through story; thus, Sandy represents Aboriginal cultural continuities that have survived continual dislocation and upheaval. Eventually, he expresses this complex, interconnected sense of identity, family and place by deciding to return home, to that 'bit of red desert'.

Anne experiences more security in her childhood than the others, yet in an important sense she lacks what Sandy has – a known family group, and place, of origin. On learning about her Aboriginal mother, Anne's sense of identity becomes less, rather than more, certain. Her confusion allows the play to engage with a typical effect of the assimilation policy, that of an identity that is in-between black and white, not quite belonging to either social group. When Anne seeks out her Aboriginal family, her white parents accuse her of betrayal, and then her black family is suspicious of her motives. The voices collectively challenge her sense of identity, asking, 'who do you think you are?' – but this is precisely what Anne is trying to figure out. In 'Anne's scene', she addresses the audience directly, indicating that her two families represent a broader social polarity that leaves many individuals with Aboriginal backgrounds caught in the middle of conflicting, and sometimes unrealistic, expectations and demands.

The experiences of *Stolen*'s characters reveal, in different ways, the dislocation and trauma that result when young children are separated from their families and prevented from having further contact with them. The play shows that people's search for a secure identity, and their desire to belong to a family, are both vital and fundamentally interconnected. The lives of Jimmy and Sandy suggest that when family ties are broken a sense of identity is elusive. On the other hand, as Anne's experiences show, when family connections can be remade, a sense of identity, though sometimes fragile and confused, can be renewed.

REFERENCES & READING

Text

Harrison, Jane, *Stolen*, Currency Press, Sydney, 2000.

Aboriginal theatre and commentary

Davis, Jack, *Barungin: Smell the Wind*, Currency Press, Sydney, 1989.

Debelle, Penelope, 'Denial fails to steal play's message', *The Age*, 4 April 2000, p.7.

Merritt, Robert, *The Cakeman*, Currency, Sydney, 1978.

Mudrooroo, 'Our World a Stage', Milli Milli Wangka: the Indigenous Literature of Australia, Hyland House, Melbourne, 1997, pp.149–163.

Shoemaker, Adam, *Black Words White Page: Aboriginal Literature 1929–1988*, University of Queensland Press, St Lucia, 1992.

Aboriginal history: the Stolen Generations

Cunneen, Chris & Liebsman, Terry, *Indigenous Peoples and the Law in Australia*, Butterworth, Sydney, 1995.

Edwards, Coral & Read, Peter, *The Lost Children*, Doubleday, Moorebank, 1989.

Haebich, Anna, *Broken Circles: Fragmenting Indigenous Families 1800–2000*, Fremantle Arts Centre Press, South Fremantle, 2000.

Human Rights and Equal Opportunity Commission (HREOC), *Bringing Them Home: the report of the national inquiry into the separation of Aboriginal and Torres Strait Islander children from their families*, Stirling Press, Sydney, 1997.

Kidd, Rosalind, *The Way We Civilise*, University of Queensland Press, St Lucia, 1997.

Moriarty, John, *Saltwater Fella*, Penguin, Victoria, 2000.

Pepper, Phillip and De Araugo, Tess, *The Kurnai of Gippsland, Hyland House*, Melbourne, 1985.

Tucker, Margaret, *If Everyone Cared*, Grosvenor, Melbourne, 1977.

Films

Australia, directed by Baz Luhrmann, 20th Century Fox, 2008.

Indigenous Law in Australia, produced by ABC/VEA, Bendigo 1999.

Kanyini, directed by Melanie Hogan, Hopscotch, 2006.

Living With Difference: Exploring Racism and Australian Identity, ABC/VEA, Bendigo, 1999.

Lousy Little Sixpence, directed by Alec Morgan, Ronin Films, 1985.

More Than Skin Deep: Racial Discrimination in Australia, produced by ABC/VEA, Bendigo, 1998.

Rabbit-Proof Fence, directed by Phillip Noyce, Miramax, 2002.

The First Australians, directed by Rachel Perkins, SBS Television, 2008.

The Stolen Generation, produced by VEA Australia with the co-operation of ABCTV Bendigo, 1998.

Website

Reconciliation Australia, http://www.reconciliation.org.au